A Theory
of Political Exchange

PRENTICE-HALL CONTEMPORARY POLITICAL THEORY SERIES

David Easton, *Editor*

R. L. CURRY, JR.
L. L. WADE

A Theory
of Political Exchange
Economic Reasoning
in Political Analysis

PRENTICE-HALL, INC., ENGLEWOOD CLIFFS, N.J.

PRENTICE-HALL INTERNATIONAL, INC., *London*
PRENTICE-HALL OF AUSTRALIA, PTY. LTD., *Sydney*
PRENTICE-HALL OF CANADA, LTD., *Toronto*
PRENTICE-HALL OF INDIA PRIVATE LTD., *New Delhi*
PRENTICE-HALL OF JAPAN, INC., *Tokyo*

Library of Congress Catalog Card Number: 68-54064

Printed in the United States of America

Current printing (last digit):
10 9 8 7 6 5 4 3 2 1

*To Aurora
and Joyce*

Preface to
Contemporary Political Theory Series

This volume is part of a new series in political science that is devoted to empirically oriented theory. Nothing testifies more eloquently to the growing strength of empirical political theory than the conviction that now, after more than twenty-five hundred years of development, it is for the first time possible to think of building a publication series out of volumes devoted exclusively to the construction of such theory. The series is itself a sign of the times; we hope it will also provide a means for vigorously and creatively reinforcing the present tendencies.

This series will contribute to the development of contemporary political theory in several distinctive ways. First and foremost, our primary objective is to gather together brief but exciting monographs that will explore alternative approaches to empirical theory. Some of these may be concerned with general, overarching theories that seek to bring order and coherence to the whole field of political science. Others may devote themselves to less comprehensive, partial theories that help to integrate selected aspects of political life, intranational, international, and cross-national. Still others may seek to explore the theoretical assumptions of existing empirical research and to systematize and assess their findings in the hope of bringing added clarity to a subfield, enhancing its theoretical relevance, and giving it a new sense of purpose and direction. Although the main emphasis will be on stimulating the production of critical and creative works that deal with the substance of theories in such areas, on occasion it will be appropriate to include volumes that direct their attention to the methodological tasks of theory construction itself.

We expect the series to leave its impact on the development of theory in a second way. It will provide a single medium through which original monographs in empirical or descriptive theory can be assembled. We would hope thereby to stimulate and reinforce the broadest range of experimentation with respect to alternative approaches to theory. Underlying the whole series is the basic premise that only through innovative and courageous efforts in a multitude of divergent and conflicting directions will it be possible for a gradual and meaningful consensus to arise in the course of time with regard to the outlines of a useful general theory or set of partial theories. It is the very essence of the theoretical enterprise that, if and when it seems appropriate, it should feel free to sever itself from the bonds of traditional ways of looking at political life. By providing an established publishing outlet, we would hope to lend encouragement in this direction at a time when it is most needed.

Third, we would hope that the availability in a single series of a growing assemblage of volumes on empirical theory will have a decisive influence on teaching and training in this field. We are in a process of transition in political science toward a more rigorous science and the series may be seen as another small effort to aid the change.

With regard to teaching and training in the function, tasks, and substance of empirical theory, a strong desire to improve the facilities in political science has not been wanting. But a major barrier has blocked the way. We have lacked a sufficient number of serious monographs to provide enough scope and depth to make formal courses in this area feasible as well as desirable. We would expect that in due time this series would offer a core around which courses on empirical theory might be initially developed, or where they already exist, enriched. In themselves such courses would contribute immeasurably to attracting the best minds in each generation of students to the field of theory or in sensitizing them to the actual function of theory in empirical research. By testifying to the challenge that theory presents and to the opportunities for empirical research, the series should, in its long range effect, reinforce empirical theory as an appropriate and adventuresome area for teaching and research.

Preface

The topic of this book is *political exchange*. Political exchange, as theory and concept, we think, is one of the central ways in which, increasingly, political scientists will come to think about politics. The task that the authors have set for themselves in this book is a limited one. Our effort has been neither to operationalize the exchange concept (an effort that will require the work of many researchers), nor to discuss all of the many problems inherent in the concept. What we have attempted to do is to deal with four central theoretical issues, or concerns, in modern political analysis.

The first concern is to treat exchange as something that is possibly *mutually* advantageous to people involved politically, even though they may be in conflict. For example, we will note that two entities may have conflicting political goals—the political "seller" wants a high "price" and the political "buyer" a low one. But it is conceivable that their exchange terms will result in putting each of them in a "better" position insofar as both are concerned. We treat these matters in our first chapter. We then qualify the potential for mutually advantageous exchange by introducing the notion of power (and some other factors). We note that the more powerful entity in any exchange will achieve the "better" terms of exchange and will be in a relatively better position vis-à-vis the less powerful entity as a consequence of the exchange. But we do not deny that power may be distributed so as to make one party less well off than he was previously, following an exchange imposed by the powerful. We consider this latter case not a matter of exchange, which is normally voluntary, but of coercion, which is not. The politically despised and dispossessed may be disenfranchised from the polity. Their fate is completely in the hands of others.

The second concern is to delineate what we regard as the major political exchange arenas, or "markets." In our second chapter, we deal with exchange as it is conducted among entities within the context of these markets and as the entities attempt to improve their political positions. We more fully delineate the participating actors, properties, and decision-making rules that interact to produce for a given polity its characteristic political structures (markets). We go on, in Chapter III, to analyze a particular market (bureaucratic recruitment) to show, first, how our methodology may be employed and, second, how exchanges work in this market.

The third concern is to analyze more fully the operation of power in political market structures. In the fourth chapter, we regard power as the singularly most important characteristic of market structures. Power is the ability to eliminate (or reduce) the number of alternatives from which others are free to choose and/or to prevent their free choice from among alternatives. The result of power is the ability of the powerful to force an exchange, at their own terms, on the powerless or less powerful. We argue that the more competitive a political market is (or the more decentralized its decision-making system), the more likely it is that the goals of social efficiency, political freedom, and social equality will be attained.

The fourth issue is to suggest an account of the process by which political output priorities are ranked and political inputs are organized and transformed into political outputs. We deal largely in Chapters IV and V not with competitive, but rather with "imperfect," political market structures, in order to account for an uneven distribution of power and other political resources. In summary, then, what we try to provide is a systematic account, first of all, of the process through which political resources (inputs) become policies (outputs) and how policies are allocated to the holders of these resources. From the point of view of certain political actors (and it will become clear why they engage our attention), we analyze the polity "backward" into the political resource markets and "forward" into the policy markets. The market activities of these actors organize the polity—they coordinate conflict. Second, we analyze the function of the power possessed by these certain actors in terms of the exchanges the actors affect in the resource and policy markets. That is, we deal with the question of who benefits from their activity—they themselves, the polity, or both. We discuss these matters in Chapter V.

Chapter VI concludes the book and contains some implications for further work suggested by our formulation of political exchange. The Selected Bibliography is organized into two sections. The first section suggests works in economic theory that might be of particular value to readers interested in improving their own skills in that field before attempting further work in political economy; the second section is intended to serve as an introduction to some of the more important literature bearing more directly on the economic analysis of politics.

This essay employs, then, certain lines of reasoning drawn from economic theory. We think such an approach is both useful and powerful, but our approach is secondary to our purpose: the notion of exchange is not dependent upon economic reasoning. It is applicable as well within the framework of alternative approaches to political analysis. For example, general systems analysis, communications theory, game theory, group theory, most theories of mass society, all involve some notions of exchange. In all formulations of the political order, people give things to others to get things for themselves. This is the process we try to understand.

The fact that we employ economic analysis in this book requires explanation. As those are aware who are familiar with the development of systematic theory in the behavioral sciences, the study of economics involves a confrontation with elegance and austerity that is unmatched in the other social disciplines. Our view is that the development of economics has shown the great felicity of approaching things in a way that is not, unfortunately, familiar to many social scientists. Our view, like that expressed by Lord Keynes in his introduction to the *Cambridge Economic Handbooks,* is that ". . . economics does not furnish a body of settled conclusions. . . . It is an apparatus of the mind, a technique of thinking, which helps its possessor to draw correct conclusions." "Economic" analysis is really just one form of social analysis, equally applicable to other arenas of human activity. It is not, as sometimes alleged, a "metaphor" that can be used to deal with some political problems. It is a basic methodological technique of investigation.

There have been some efforts to examine politics from the perspective of economic theory. One of our purposes is to contribute to this emerging genre. We hope to provide those students of social and political theory who are not acquainted with economic theory and methodology with an axiomatic view of politics derived from intermediate economic theory. No formal knowledge of economics is necessary to read this volume, although it would certainly be helpful. We explain the economic theory, methodology, and graphical analysis that we employ. Our effort is to make clear the basic fecundity of thinking in terms of economic theory. To the student of economic theory we do not pretend to teach economics. We do, however, attempt to suggest a wider basis for the use of his analytical tools and methodological approach.

This volume stems from an exchange relationship between an economist (Curry) and a political scientist (Wade), both of whom are hopeful that the results are more fruitful than would have been any effort to deal separately with the thesis presented in the following pages. We are grateful to our colleagues, both economists and political scientists, who have read this book, or portions of it, during its preparatory stage. Their efforts have saved us from errors we would otherwise have committed. Our thanks are due also to James J. Murray, III, Assistant Vice President of Prentice-Hall, to Professor William Riker, and to Professor David Easton, Editor of the Prentice-Hall series in Contemporary Political Theory. Our special intellectual debt is to Professor William C. Mitchell, whose understanding of, and contributions to, systematic political theory have greatly interested and influenced us. We alone, of course, assume responsibility for what is contained herein.

R. L. C., Jr.
L. L. W.

Table of Contents

ONE

*Exchange in Political
and Economic Analysis*

The polity may be conceived of as a large and complex system of decisions and decision-makers. We will take it as reasonable in this essay to assume that people *act* in accordance with their decisions. The decision-makers may usefully be classified as *policy-seekers* and as *policy-makers*. In this book, all of the decision-makers are taken to be *individuals,* although they may act for, or in the name of, a group. We refer to policy-seekers as decision-makers because we are concerned to understand the decisions that they make in pursuit of public policies. Most decision-makers normally act in a variety of more discrete capacities (to be explained later); we will therefore be able to introduce greater precision into the discussion at another point. To understand the polity as a system of *exchange* decisions, it is necessary to understand how political decisions are made, as well as the consequences implied by the interaction of these decisions. The task of this book is to contribute to that understanding.

The scheme of decision-making assumed here is quite simple: a typical political decision either implicitly or explicitly involves an element of exchange; that is, an individual has to give up something in order to get some-

1

thing. The thing given up is a *cost* and the thing obtained leads to a *reward* of some sort. We also assume that an individual will do the best that he can in any exchange (although we need not assume the maximizing individual of certain economic theories), given the resources with which he starts. The problem for any individual, then, is to allocate, or "spend," his resources in such a way as to reach the most preferred position possible. In all cases the political actors have to operate with limited resources. The usual decision made by any political actor, then, is to try to improve his position with respect to the things that he wants, subject to the constraints of limited resources, limited information (including his ability to "handle" information), and the political conditions (rules and properties) of the polity in which he must operate. The sum total of such decisions determines what happens in a polity.

EXCHANGE DECISIONS

As we say, a political decision is often (although not always) an exchange decision. One has to balance what he can get against what he has to forgo in order to get it. Consider a policy-seeker trying to obtain a set of public policies available at a given cost per policy "unit" (about which more later). The more policy units he attempts to secure, the more resources he must allocate to someone else. He must decide how many policy units to demand, considering what he has to give up in order to make an exchange.

Thus, there are two elements involved in any exchange decision: (1) How much of a policy (or reward), available at a given cost, does one want? (2) How much is one willing to give up in order to get it? In economics the first decision would be described as the *demand* element in the exchange and the second decision as the *supply* (or cost) element. Both questions must be answered by the policy-makers as well as by the policy-seekers. To understand political exchange, then, we have to analyze these two elements of the situation from the viewpoints of the various individuals involved in exchange.

How should (or, we assume, does) a self-interested policy-seeker make an exchange decision? If the cost of any available policy is known, he has to answer the following question: Does what the policy-seeker gets as a result of an exchange give him greater satisfaction, or lead him to a more preferred position, than having the thing that he would give up in order to make the exchange? If the answer is "Yes" to this question, then he would gain by making the exchange. And still further, he should be willing to make the exchange as long as the answer to the question is in the affirmative. These very simple notions, we hope to show, make it possible to say some interesting things about politics. We must now, however, explain more precisely certain terms that we will employ throughout this essay.

THE DIVISIBILITY OF POLICY ALTERNATIVES

Policy is the term given for a state of affairs either desired or pursued by someone; policies are the generic commodities available in polity. This view is fully consistent with other analyses, for example, David Easton's statement that politics consists in the "authoritative allocation of values for a whole society."[1] We are concerned to know how this allocation works and we assume that Easton means something very close to "policy" by the term "values." Policies, then, are the values for which political actors bargain and compete and are distinguished from extra-polity policies by their authoritative character. (We do not exclude coercion from political analysis by the terms "bargain" and "compete." These latter processes occur within a structure, or situation, that may well involve power and coercion. This point will become clear as the analysis proceeds.) If the politicians (policy-makers) determine that individuals receiving full social security benefits may not earn more than $1200 per year without a reduction in receipts from the government, the politicians are pursuing a policy that can be, and presumably is, enforced by the authoritative monopoly of coercion they possess. But the point we make here is that such a policy is *divisible*. Policies are rarely permanent—thus the government may choose to increase, decrease, or remove the earning limit for social security recipients. It is in this sense that most policies are divisible. One may have more or less than whatever it is that current policy does in the way of allocating things people want. For example, conservationists do not only secure National Parks from the polity; they receive parks of different sizes and locations, containing various geological and scenic values—National Historical Parks, National Monuments, wilderness areas, camping sites in the national forests—all of which vary in dimension and importance to those people interested in such things. Public highways are clearly divisible in the same sense, as are military forces, taxes, maritime subsidies, welfare programs, government controls over business, public jobs, and all other public policies and programs that occur to us. True, atomic reactors may require a minimum size and investment, but if the government is interested in the more generic policy question concerning home lighting systems, it may allocate kerosene lanterns, or even candles; it is this that is meant by the divisibility of policies. The same is true for less tangible policies, as, for instance,

[1] Easton advances this definition in "An Approach to the Analysis of Political Systems," *World Politics,* IX (1956–57), p. 381, and has used it consistently in his extensive monographic work.

civil rights. Civil rights involve the vote (clearly divisible in any number of ways, ranging from the establishment of racial, sexual, property, or age criteria, or even by giving some individuals more votes than others), freedom of speech (divisible in terms of who is free to speak, in what forum, at what length, and on which topics), assembly (divisible in any number of obvious ways), and other values similarly divisible.

We are suggesting here that, when the government sets out to divide the social pie, it is free within policy areas to reduce any given piece of any given policy to extraordinarily refined dimensions. That the government has this competence—supplied to it by the structure of the polity—is important in political analysis, although it is rarely stated explicitly. The divisibility of policies enables one to develop the notion of policy "units," or slices of whatever size and scope, of policies, and further, enables one to say something about the comparability, the relative evaluation, of policy units. It also enables one to think of public policies as continuous variables; that is, policy or reward variables that can continuously take on new values. We will use this concept throughout this book. The use of continuous variables is most fruitful analytically, even though only economists among social scientists have built their theories around them.

Assuming that policies are *not* divisible makes the point: conceive of the government choosing between an interstate highway system and a missile defense system. Without the divisibility principle, there would be no basis upon which, given limited resources, to decide the magnitude of resources to be allocated in pursuit of either policy. Why X rather than X_1 number of highway miles, and why Y rather than Y_1 number of missiles, or, for that matter, why Z rather than Z_1 Vista Volunteers? The existential levels settled upon in each case, we would suggest, involve the implicit use of the divisibility principle (and, as we show below, the indifference principle).

UTILITY THEORY: IN ECONOMICS

In this essay we will want to borrow certain ideas from economic theory to deal with the problem of political exchange. In this section we will introduce some additional rather basic ideas from economics, try to explain them, and then show how they might be applied in a theory of political exchange.

The concepts of *specialization* and *exchange* are basic to that portion of economic theory devoted to the analysis of microeconomic behavior. We shall, however, appropriate only those concepts from the general corpus of microeconomic theory that are relevant to our analysis of political behavior. We will not, therefore, discuss all aspects of specialization or even exchange, as those terms are used in economics. Marshall defined this aspect of economic theory as ". . . that part of the Social Science of man's actions in society, which deals with his Efforts to satisfy his Wants, insofar as the efforts and wants are capable of being measured in terms of wealth, or its general representative, i.e., money."[2] We believe that aspects of this part of social science can be used even when the money measure is lacking.[3]

We shall outline the manner by which economic theory has analyzed human behavior as it relates to an individual's efforts to maximize his wants (or utility or satisfaction) and to minimize his efforts in doing so. However, we must reiterate that we shall use only the concepts relevant to our later efforts, rather than those discussed in the development of economic theory.

Let us consider the theory of individual behavior, first through the older cardinal *utility* approach,[4] and then through the more modern *indifference* analysis.[5] The two approaches are, for the most part, different ways of explaining identical phenomena. Utility theory is based on the notion that an individual gains utility (or satisfaction) from the consumption of goods and services (or rewards). This seems to be a reasonable

[2] Alfred Marshall, *Principles of Economics,* (9th ed.; New York: Macmillan, 1961), p. 49. The *Principles* was first published in 1890.

[3] Modified in this way, Marshall's statement would serve as a definition of the new economic sociology represented in such works as Peter Blau, *Exchange and Power in Social Life* (New York: John Wiley & Sons, 1964); George C. Homans, *Social Behavior: Its Elementary Forms* (New York: Harcourt, Brace & World, 1961); John W. Thibault and Harold H. Kelley, *The Social Psychology of Groups* (New York: John Wiley & Sons, 1959); and an often overlooked but quite extraordinary book by George K. Zipf, *Human Behavior and the Principle of Least Effort* (Cambridge, Mass.: Addison-Wesley, 1949), which, among other things, deals with the question of efficiency.

[4] See Paul A. Samuelson, *Economics,* (7th ed.; New York: McGraw-Hill, 1967), pp. 417–423; Richard H. Leftwich, *The Price System and Resource Allocation* (New York: Holt, Rinehart & Winston, 1966), pp. 47–65; Charles E. Ferguson, *Microeconomic Theory* (Homewood, Ill.: Richard D. Irwin, 1966), pp. 14–15; Kalman J. Cohen and Richard M. Cyert, *Theory of the Firm* (Englewood Cliffs, N.J.: Prentice-Hall, 1965), pp. 29–31; William J. Baumol, *Economic Theory and Operations Analysis* (Englewood Cliffs, N.J.: Prentice-Hall, 1965), pp. 180–182. These few sources do not exhaust the materials delineating the theoretical approaches that we have expropriated from the corpus of intermediate microeconomic theory. We have provided these sources (and others, in the Bibliography) for the student who may wish assistance in mastering these concepts. We suggest that the beginning student start with Samuelson's book and then Leftwich's before moving on to the others. We do not intend here to contribute to the development of economic theory. Rather, we present certain theoretical points that we will use later.

[5] Samuelson, *op. cit.,* pp. 429–431; Leftwich, *op. cit.,* pp. 66–71; Ferguson, *op. cit.,* pp. 19–24; George J. Stigler, *The Theory of Price* (New York: Macmillan, 1966), pp. 46–53; Cohen and Cyert, *op. cit.,* pp. 79–81; Baumol, *op. cit.,* pp. 183–188.

assumption. Total utility is the total amount of satisfaction obtained from obtaining various quantities of rewards. This is a less reasonable assumption and we will depart from it to some extent later. The more of a reward obtained per unit of time, the greater the total utility (or satisfaction) any individual will receive up to a certain point. At some level of total utility, rewards will reach a maximum; the individual will not be capable of enjoying any greater satisfaction from a given reward even though more is thrust upon him. He is saturated with that *particular* reward.

A hypothetical total utility curve showing the situation depicted above is drawn in Figure 1-1. The point of saturation is reached at a level of six units of X per unit of time. Up to that point, total utility increases as consumption increases. Then, total utility decreases.

Figure 1-1.

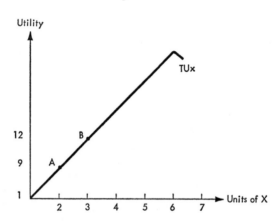

Marginal utility is defined as the change in total utility coming from a one-unit change in the quantity of rewards obtained that yield utility. In Figure 1-1, if the individual has two units per unit of time and increases his acquisition to three, his total utility would increase from nine to twelve units of utility. Marginal utility of the third unit is thus three units of utility. Marginal utility of the third unit is approximate to the average slope of the total utility curve between points A and B. The slope of the total utility curve between points A and B reflects an increase in utility resulting from a one-unit increase in consumption. It is equal to 3/1 if the relevant segment of the curve is presumed to be a straight line. The total utility curve is not a straight line. However, the error involved in assuming it so becomes progressively smaller as the distance between the points decreases. E.g., if the distance on the X axis that measures one unit of X is very small, marginal utility at any given level of consumption is equal to the slope of the corresponding point on the total utility curve. Since marginal utility is the change in total utility from one-unit increments in rewards, a marginal revenue curve is plotted as in Figure 1-2.

Figure 1-2.

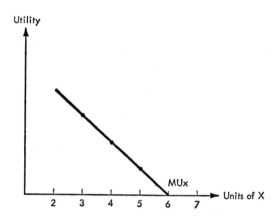

In economic theory, the concept of utility aids in explaining the behavior of the individual consumer in the market place. The explanation presumes rational action (about which more later) by individuals (actors) to achieve certain objectives, subject to certain limitations imposed upon them. The objective postulated for the rational economic actor is maximization of the amount of utility (or satisfaction) that he can obtain from his given and limited resources. His preferences are shown by his utility curve, given its determinants at any particular moment in time are given. His problem is to decide how much to obtain of *each* of the many *different* rewards so as to secure the highest possible level of total utility with his available resources. The limitations he faces in maximizing satisfaction are his available resources and the costs of the rewards he wishes to obtain. His resources are fixed per time period, and he is unable to influence the costs of most rewards he obtains. Limited, then, by his resources and by costs, he attempts to maximize his utility (or satisfaction). These assumptions must be kept in mind when we discuss political exchange. We will emphasize them later to make their relevance clear.

Assume that an individual obtains two rewards, X and Y, the costs of which are P_x and P_y. We consider P_x and P_y fixed; resource units of X or resource units of Y represent a certain quantity of X or Y, just as would any other quantity that we might measure. Assume that the individual's resources are limited so that he must allocate them in such a fashion so as to maximize utility (or satisfaction).

In order to deal with the individual's allocation problem, it will be convenient to put in simple equations the conditions necessary for maximizing satisfaction. At any level, the marginal utility per unit of X divided by the price (or cost) of X, or MU_x/P_x, is the marginal utility per dollar's worth of X. Similarly, the marginal utility per unit of Y at any level divided by the price (or cost) of Y, or MU_y/P_y, can be read as the marginal utility per dollar's worth of Y. The conditions necessary for maximizing satisfaction will be

$$\frac{MU_x}{P_x} = \frac{MU_y}{P_y} = \frac{MU_z}{P_z} = \cdots \frac{MU_n}{P_n}$$

However, this does not take into account the resource restraint under which the individual operates. The total expenditure of the actor cannot exceed his resources, which we show as R. His total expenditure on reward X is equal to the price (or cost) of X multiplied by the quantity purchased. The same holds for each other reward obtained. The resource restraint can be expressed as follows:

$$x \times P_x + y \times P_y + z \times P_z + \ldots n \times P_n = R$$

Economic activity consists basically of exchange among individuals. Through the money system, goods are exchanged for goods, resources are exchanged for goods, and resources are exchanged for resources. But money is not at all the only social exchange medium. Money and other things get exchanged in the polity through much the same processes as they do in the economy. It is also a mistake to assume that one of the parties in an exchange transaction must be the gainer while the other must be the loser. In exchange of goods among individuals, all parties to the exchange might increase their satisfaction. The prospect of gain causes voluntary exchange to occur, even though the structure of the market may contain inequitable elements, and one individual's gain may be proportionately higher than another's.

For exchange to occur, two or more individuals must place different relative values on the rewards involved. Thus, contrary to some views, not all economic exchange grows out of something having a common money value alone, but out of different valuations placed upon something by individuals. This is not "quantifiable" in the same way that money is. Thus, economic exchange is much more like the other forms of social exchange than is sometimes realized. Relative values of rewards by a single individual depend upon the relative marginal utilities of his rewards and their money or resource costs. Thus, for all holders of rewards to be in *equilibrium* (which only means that no incentive to exchange exists), each individual's holding of a reward must be such that the ratio of the marginal utility per unit of cost of any reward for him is the same as it is for all other rewards he acquires. For individual **A** to be in "equilibrium," MU_x/MU_y must equal MU_x/MU_y, etc. When these conditions do not hold, it becomes worthwhile for the individual to seek to alter the terms of exchange and to engage in exchange until it does hold. However, this presumes that utility can be measured. In fact, it has not been, perhaps cannot be, so measured. But it does not have to be.

For the most part, *we will abandon the idea that satisfactions can be measured cardinally and added, and we will use indifference analysis to deal with the rational behavior of individuals in place of this type of analysis.* The assumption that the individual tries to maximize his well-being is retained. But *maximizing satisfaction no longer means achieving the largest sum total of satisfaction, but rather reaching a more preferred position.* This approach avoids certain insoluble problems and introduces greater conceptual relevance vis-à-vis the analysis of political exchange.

UTILITY THEORY: IN POLITICS

Given the above explanation of utility theory in economics, we will now illustrate a similar conception in political analysis. We may assume that political actors seek utility in the same way that economic actors do and that they attempt, therefore, to make exchange decisions in such a way as to get more rewards than they currently have. Normally, as the above analysis shows, we assume that more units of any value will yield more satisfaction than some lesser amount, but that the amount of satisfaction will increase in smaller proportions given an increase in the number of policy units secured. The analysis will be a very simple one but the principle is important.

Consider the question: How many policy units should a self-interested political actor invest in securing? To answer this, the policy-seeker must weigh the utility of the policy units sought and the utility of the resources that he must give up to get them. Should he buy at least two units rather than one? Here he must weigh the additional utility that he gets in securing two policy units rather than one and the additional utility lost from giving up the resources necessary to obtain two units rather than one.

He must weigh these factors for all decision situations in which policy units are obtained and for which resources are spent. We show this for decision situation A through N in the equation below, where R stands for resources expended and MU for the marginal utilities involved.

$$\frac{MU_a}{R_a} = \frac{MU_b}{R_b} \cdot \cdot \cdot = \frac{MU_n}{R_n}$$

Economists, of course, deal with resources expressed in monetary terms. But this is only a convention, albeit a very useful one. In fact, we can express the same idea in terms of any type of marginal valuations placed on anything that people are interested in, regardless of the index of valuation used. It makes no difference whether the index is money, social approval, power, respect, or any other individual or social value.

Before abandoning marginal utility theory for indifference analysis, we will employ it again to emphasize its potential application in political science. The assumption states that, as a political actor considers securing more policy units, or rewards, the marginal utility associated with a greater number of units declines. Thus, for instance, as farmers secure more policy units from policy-makers, say roads, the value of the nth road will be less than the value of the first, or the sixth, if the nth road is any road in excess of six. This obviously assumes that all the roads are the same in terms of whatever intrinsic service they are able to yield to the farmers. Now let us return to the problem and assume that the principle of diminishing marginal utility is applicable to the policy in question. Let us agree that the policy has to do with county roads and county schools. The political actors—farmers—are faced with the problem of having to decide how many roads to secure from the county politicians. Suppose that each farmer's resources are fixed in quantity. As they consider securing more roads, for each actor, the marginal utility of roads declines; thus, the more roads secured, the lower their marginal utility. As each considers securing more rather than fewer roads, a point will be reached at which the marginal utility of an additional road divided by the cost of obtaining it is equal to the marginal utility of another classroom divided by its resource cost (taxes). Assume that the farmers have a fixed resource base to allocate to both roads and schools and that the cost of any road and any school in question are equal. We could apply the divisibility principle and talk in terms of classrooms as against miles of roads (or school playgrounds as against road repairs), but will not do so in order to simplify the point we are making. Their decision problem is to pick a combination of roads and schools that they can obtain from a fixed resource base and that would give them the greatest satisfaction. We are now discussing the aggregate utilities of all farmers rather than the utility of any particular farmer; the problem is dealt with later but need not concern us here. Once again we assume that the principle of diminishing marginal utility is applicable to both values in question. The answer for the problem we have posed is for the farmers to allocate their resources in such a way that the marginal utility of schools is equal to the marginal utility of roads. That is, they should choose a combination of roads and schools that they could obtain by allocating all of their resources so that the utility per unit of resource cost derived from the last school built is equal to that obtained from the last road built.

To demonstrate that this gives the farmers maximum utility, assume that they have secured roads and schools for which marginal utilities per units of cost are *not* equal—that for roads it is greater than for shcools. The question raised here is whether, under these circumstances, they can improve their positions by giving up schools and substituting roads. Thus, if they secure one less school they can purchase one more road. Assuming that schools and roads have identical resource costs, such a procedure would clearly improve their position because the added utility of an additional road is greater than the utility of the foregone school. In this manner the procedure of shifting will continue until the marginal utilities of roads and schools per unit of cost are identical. At some point it will no longer be rational to make any more shifts. At that point the farmers will have done as well as they possibly could. This is an example of the marginal principle at work in the polity. It is one of the ways in which people often think about politics, even if they are not always explicitly aware of it. In general, then, the theory holds that actors will allocate any fixed quantity of something among alternative uses in such a way as to maximize their aggregate utility as well as in such a way that their marginal valuation per units of cost of their various policy or reward units will be equal. A great deal of political analysis may be undertaken with this general approach by examining the implications of decision-making situations in which this rule is applied in one form or another.

But a better way of dealing with problems such as the one just discussed is given below. Marginal analysis, whether applied to economy or polity, assumes that it is possible to measure the satisfaction that people receive from exchange. But it is not necessary, as we have said, to assume that utilities can be summed and measured accurately. Some efforts in economics make it possible to approach individual decision-making systematically and deductively without assuming maximization of interests (as commonly defined) or the precise measurability of satisfactions. We refer to indifference analysis, to which the discussion now turns.

INDIFFERENCE ANALYSIS: IN ECONOMY AND POLITY

Let us assume for the moment a world in which there are only two rewards, X and Y, for one individual. As far as the rewards are concerned, the individual's satisfaction now depends on the amounts of X and Y he can acquire. We now draw a contour line on a graph, as in Figure 1-3, in which the two coordinates represent amounts of X and Y. Any two points on one such contour line represent *collections* of rewards that are *equally* satisfactory to the individual. In order to draw such a contour line, we take a given collection of rewards, represented by a point A on the graph, and presume that the individual is indifferent between and among all other possible points or collections, B, C, D, etc., and collection A.

Figure 1-3.

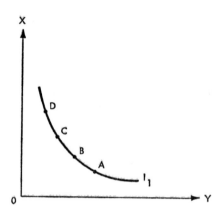

Since the indifference curve technique has been integrated into economics, it has become a standard part of economic theory. Indifference analysis provides an alternative and a supplement to the utility explanation of individual economic (and political) behavior. Economists reject as impossible the quantifying of utility. Indifference analysis eliminates the necessity of making any assumptions regarding the cardinal measurability of utility. Thus, having introduced this measurability concept, we must now at least partially discard it in favor of an ordinal measure of utility.

An indifference curve presents a picture of an individual's tastes and preferences. We assume limited choices between two commodities— rewards X and Y. The indifference curve of an individual (a consumer in economics, a policy, or a reward-seeker in politics) is obtained by presenting to the individual a range of choices among various possible combinations of X and Y. The assumption upon which indifference analysis is based is that the individual can differentiate between the combinations that yield the same satisfaction to him (and toward which he is indifferent) and those that yield greater or lesser satisfaction. The single indifference curve shows the different combinations of X and Y that yield equal satisfaction to the individual and about which he is indifferent. Assume, for example, that it makes no difference to an individual which of the combinations shown in Figure 1-3 he can attain. These combinations are points on an indifference curve.

TABLE 1-1

Points	Units X	Units Y
A	6	14
B	7	10
C	8	7
D	9	3

In Figure 1-3, units of X per unit of time are measured on the ordinate and units of Y per unit of time are measured on the abscissa. The combinations are plotted and joined to form an indifference curve, I_1. Greater amounts of satisfaction than that obtained on indifference curve I_1 are shown by a higher indifference curve in Figure 1-4, curve I_2.

Figure 1-4.

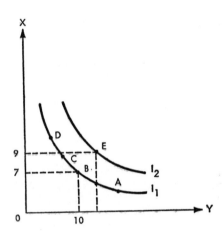

Combination B in Figure 1-4 contains 7 units of X and 10 units of Y. If we add two units of X and two of Y to combination B, we have combination E, containing 9 units of X and 12 units of Y. Since it contains more X and more Y, combination E will yield greater satisfaction to an individual than will combination A, or other combinations equivalent to A, such as B, C, and D. Innumerable indifference curves can be drawn on the diagram depicting all degrees of satisfaction. All combinations on one indifference curve are equally satisfying to an individual. All combinations on higher indifference curves are preferable to those lying on lower indifference curves. *We make no further inferences regarding the amount of satisfaction gained in moving from a lower to a higher indifference curve.*

A family of indifference curves, or an indifference map, has three basic characteristics: First, the indifference curves slope downward and to the right; second, they are convex toward the origin; and third, they are nonintersecting. The important parts of indifference curves are those which slope downward to the right. A horizontally structured indifference curve would mean that the individual is indifferent as between two combinations, both of which contain the same amount of Y, but one of which contains a greater amount of X than the other. This could occur only if the individual were saturated with it; that is, additional units of X alone would add nothing to his total satisfaction. If an indifference curve were vertical, it would mean that the two combinations of X and Y, both with the same amount of X but with one containing more Y than the other, yield equivalent satisfaction to the individual. This can occur only if the individual has reached a saturation point for Y. Usually, if an individual's satisfaction remains constant, he gives up units of one commodity (or policy) and the loss must be compensated for by additional units of another commodity (or policy). The result, shown graphically, is an indifference curve sloping, as we say, downward and to the right.

Indifference curves are also convex toward the origin, or the zero intercept. We must introduce the concept of the marginal rate of substitution of one good or policy for another to explain this phenomenon. The reader may recall that this notion was discussed in the section on utility theory in politics; here, however, we must be somewhat more precise because the idea will be with us for much of the rest of the book. The marginal rate of substitution of X for Y (MRS_{xy}) is defined as the amount of Y the individual is just willing to give up to get an additional unit of X. In Figure 1-5, suppose an individual is taking 14 units of Y and 6 units of X (on indifference curve I_1, at point A). To move to 8 units of X he would just be willing to give up consumption of 7 units of Y (point B). Thus, the marginal rate of substitution is 7/2. The more Y and the less X the individual has, the more important any unit of X is to him as compared to a unit of Y. Therefore, at point A in Figure 1-5, he would be willing to give up a considerable amount of Y to get an additional unit of X. At point B he has a large amount of X and very little Y; hence a unit of Y would be more important to him as compared with a unit of X than it was at point A, and he would be willing to give up very little of Y to get an additional unit of X. The X axis is marked off in equal quantity units between A and B. At point A the indifference curve shows that the individual is willing to give up some of Y to get an additional unit of X. As he moves from point A toward point B he acquires more of X per unit of time and less of Y. The importance of a unit of Y becomes progressively greater as compared to the importance of a unit of X. The amount of Y he is just willing to exchange to get additional units of X becomes progressively

Figure 1-5.

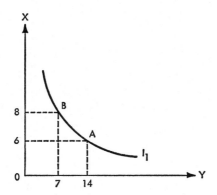

smaller. The marginal rate of substitution of X for Y is decreasing. If so, then the indifference curve must be convex toward the origin.

Indifference curves do not intersect and this is shown by examining the indifference curves of Figure 1-4. The combinations of X and Y shown on indifference curve I_2 are preferred to the combinations on indifference curve I_1. The combinations on indifference curve I_1 are equivalent to each other. Similarly, the combinations on indifference curve I_2 are also equivalent to each other. Each combination on indifference curve I_2 contains greater amounts of both X and Y than corresponding combinations on indifference curve I_1. The definition of indifference curves precludes their intersecting because indifference curve I_2 must lie above and to the right of indifference curve I_1.

We have just presented an analysis of what an individual is *willing* to do with respect to different combinations of X and Y. But what he is *able* to do depends upon the respective costs of rewards X and Y and the individual's resources.[6] These factors are put into what is sometimes referred to as a line of attainable combinations. This line of attainable combinations, when tangent to an individual's indifference curve, will show the combinations of X and Y that he can obtain and that he will prefer to all other combinations which he might obtain. As we have noted, the individual's cost factors are the costs of X and Y, and the individual's resources. The individual regards these as fixed at the moment. Suppose the individual's resources (R_1) are, to revert to an economic rather than to a political example, $300 per unit of time in value, the cost of Y is $3 per unit

[6] Samuelson, *op. cit.,* p. 431; Leftwich, *op. cit.,* pp. 72–73; Ferguson, *op. cit.,* pp. 26–31; Stigler, *op. cit.,* pp. 53–55; Cohen and Cyert, *op. cit.,* pp. 68–69; Baumol, *op. cit.,* pp. 188–190.

(Cy_1), and the cost of X is \$6 per unit (Cx_1). Figure 1-6 shows that, if the individual should allocate all of his resources on Y, he could attain 100 units of Y, or he could attain 50 units of X if he were to spend all of his income on X. A straight line joining these two points shows the alternative combinations of X and Y that the individual can attain. This is the line we refer to as the line of attainable combinations. It might also be called a resource line, a political resource line, a budget line, or a political tactic line. We will show later how a line of attainable combinations can be used in a variety of ways to increase political understanding. We simply note here that the concept has a number of potential uses.

Figure 1-6.

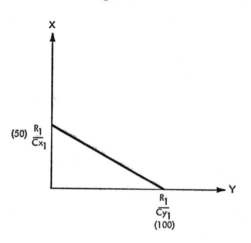

Assume that an individual's economic resource value is R_1. The cost of X is Cx_1 and the cost of Y is Cy_1. If he should spend all of his resources on Y, R_1/Cy_1 in Figure 1-6 shows the total number of units of Y that he might obtain. If he were to spend all of his income on X, R_1/Cx_1 shows the number of units of X that he could purchase. The line of attainable combinations joins the two extreme points. The slope of the line of attainable combinations is:

$$\frac{R_1/Cy_1}{R_1/Cx_1} = \frac{R_1}{Cy_1} \times \frac{Cx_1}{R_1} = \frac{Cx_1}{Cy_1}$$

The individual's indifference curves and his line of attainable combinations are brought together in Figure 1-7.[7] It shows that he can allocate

---

[7] Samuelson, *op. cit.*, p. 432; Leftwich, *op. cit.*, pp. 73–75; Ferguson, *op. cit.*, pp. 32–34; Stigler, *op. cit.*, pp. 55–68; Cohen and Cyert, *op. cit.*, pp. 69–71; Baumol, *op. cit.*, pp. 182–192.

resources between X and Y in a manner so as to move to his more pre-ferred position. The indifference curves show what he would like to do, and the line of attainable combinations shows what he can do. The individual can take any combination, such as H, I, E, F, or G, that lies on the line of attainable combinations. However, he would not take combination H be-cause I is also available to him and it is on a higher indifference curve. Combination E is on a still higher indifference curve, but combinations F and G are on lower indifference curves. Combination I will give the individ-ual a higher level of satisfaction than will any other combination allowable with his resources and the given costs of X and Y. The individual maxi-mizes his satisfaction by taking that combination of X and Y where his line of attainable combinations is tangent to an indifference curve. The indiffer-ence curve to which the line of attainable combinations is tangent is the highest one he can reach. He will take x_1 of X and y_1 of Y.

Figure 1-7.

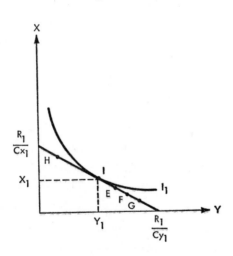

Now the factors that give rise to exchanges among or between individ-uals can be analyzed in terms of indifference analysis. This is the heart of this essay, because we are most interested in exchange and not just the preferences of individuals. The preferences are prelude, although they have in fact been the focus of most contemporary empirical research. The next step is to deal systematically with exchanges that grow out of preferences. This has not been the focus of current political research, although we would argue that it should be.

Consider two individuals, A and B, each of whom holds stocks of, and consumes, two utilities giving rewards X and Y. Individual A's preferences for X and Y are shown on the conventional portion of Figure 1-8.[8] The indifference map of B is rotated and imposed on that of A so that the axes of the two diagrams form a box.

Figure 1-8.

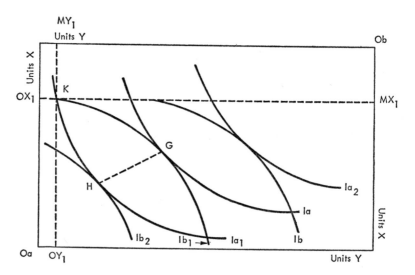

The indifference curves of A are convex to O_a while those of B are convex to O_b. Any point on or in the rectangle represents a possible distribution of the values X and Y between the two individuals. The initial distribution of X and Y is represented by point K, which lies within the rectangle formed by the two sets of axes. Individual A holds Oy_1 of Y and B holds My_1. The amount of X held by A is Ox_1 and that held by B is Mx_1. Individual A is on indifference curve Ia_1. For A, the marginal rate of substitu-

<hr>

[8] See especially Leftwich, *op. cit.,* pp. 75–77. At this point we are involved in an area of economic theory referred to as "welfare economics." It does not, of course, refer to institutional forms of welfare transfers. Rather, it involves a highly sophisticated discussion of principles by which, hopefully, the conditions that maximize human welfare can be discovered. It is beyond the scope of this volume to deal with formal welfare economics, but should a reader wish to examine this set of concepts, we suggest that he refer to Baumol's excellent treatment in Chapter 16 of his previously cited volume. The bibliography that Baumol includes in this chapter refers to other works. The first nine chapters in I. M. D. Little's *Critique of Welfare Economics* (London: Oxford University Press, 1958) would be excellent for intensive study. A succinct and manageable outline of welfare economics is presented in Francis M. Bator's article, "The Simple Analytics of Welfare Maximization," *American Economic Review,* XLVII (March 1957), pp. 22–59.

tween A and B. Nor do we attempt to deal with the possibility that further exchange from any point on the contract curve might either (1) make both better off or (2) make one better off and the other no less well off.[9]

POLITICAL INDIFFERENCE: AN ILLUSTRATION

One of the best-tested statements in political science asserts that social class, income, education, and other scarce social values are all related to political participation.[10] The higher one stands with respect to these values, the more likely that he will participate in political activity. Why this should be the case is a matter of some dispute. Some analysts argue (1) that those with greater social resources have more at stake (more to lose) potentially, and thus more to get politically exercised about, or (2) it could not be otherwise in large-scale societies.[11] Others assert that, logically, those who possess least of what there is to get should, or should be expected to, participate more politically in an effort to secure more of whatever it is they lack.[12] Indifference analysis may be used to relate the social resources that people have with how they will behave politically. Briefly, political behavior may be explained in part by examining the effect of personal resource changes (e.g., changes in class, income, education) upon political behavior, as well as the effect of a change in the cost of some policies on the demand for others.

Suppose that an individual's resource base is given and fixed and that he has to allocate all of it in securing two public policies (which, it will be recalled, are divisible into policy units). How will he react to a change in the availability, or cost, of the policies? How will he react to a change in his social position, that is, his resource base? Examine Figure 1-9, which

[9] There are treatments of these points in Little, *op. cit.*, Chapter 6.

[10] The literature on the variable rates of political participation is inexhaustible. Particularly relevant studies concerned with a variety of political contexts, or markets, include Seymour M. Lipset, Paul F. Lazarsfeld, Allen H. Barton, and Juan Linz, "The Psychology of Voting: An Analysis of Political Behavior." in Gardner Lindzey (ed.), *Handbook of Social Psychology* (Cambridge: Addison-Wesley, 1954), II, pp. 1124–1175; Robert E. Lane, *Political Life: Why People Get Involved in Politics* (Glencoe, Ill.: The Free Press, 1959); Lester W. Milbrath, *Political Participation*, (Chicago: Rand McNally, 1965); Gabriel A. Almond and Sidney Verba, *The Civic Culture* (Princeton: Princeton University Press, 1963); James C. Davies, *Human Nature in Politics* (New York: John Wiley & Sons, 1963); Robert Agger, Daniel Goldrich, and Bert Swanson, *The Rulers and the Ruled* (New York: John Wiley & Sons, 1964).

[11] See Gaetano Mosca, *The Ruling Class* (New York: McGraw Hill, 1939), and Vilfredo Pareto, *The Mind and Society*, ed. Arthur Livingston (New York: Harcourt, Brace, 1935).

[12] See Lane' statement in *op. cit.*, Chapter 22. Also relevant is Peter Bachrach, *The Theory of Democratic Elitism* (Boston: Little, Brown, 1967), especially Chapter 7.

tion of X for Y at point K is greater than it is for B. Individual B is indifference curve Ib_1. Individual A is willing to exchange more X to get additional unit of Y than B needs to convince him to exchange the unit of

The individual (or individuals) gain from exchange when the init holdings of the two commodities or policies are indicated by a point which an indifference curve of A cuts through an indifference curve of I With K showing the initial distribution of X and Y, exchanges of X by in dividual A to individual B for Y could occur in a manner whereby indif ference curve Ib_1 is followed downward to the right. Individual B is mad no worse off, but individual A reaches a "more preferred position" until the distribution of rewards between the two is represented by point G, at which indifference curve I_a is tangent to indifference curve I_b; no further exchange can occur without making one party, or both parties, worse off than they are at G. Individual B could exchange Y to individual A for X in such a way that indifference curve I_{a1} is followed downward to the right. Such exchanges leave A no worse off than before but place B in successively "more preferred positions" until the distribution of goods is that represented by point H, at which indifference curve I_{a1} is tangent to indifference curve I_{b2}.

There are several distributions of the two rewards between A and B at which there is no further reason to exchange. The possibile equilibrium distributions are traced out along GH, a line (contact curve) formed by the points of tangency of A's indifference curves with those of B, the relevant position of the curve being between G and H. The distribution of X and Y on the contract curve at which the parties would ultimately arrive depends upon their respective bargaining strengths, skills, and resources. If A is stronger in terms of these factors, the distribution of goods will be nearer point G; if B is stronger, it will be nearer point H.

The condition necessary for an equilibrium distribution of rewards between A and B is that the maximum amount of X that individual A is willing to exchange to get an additional unit of Y is equal to the minimum amount of X that B would accept in exchange for a unit of Y. No gain from further exchange would benefit *both* parties. This equilibrium could occur at any point between G and H. Formal "welfare economics" refers to all such points as *Pareto Optimums*. That is, once a point on the contract curve is reached, any movement along the curve will make someone better off but at the expense of making someone else less well off. Our purpose here has been to make only one point: It is possible for the two entities to move from point F to some other point on the contract curve between G and H and, as a consequence, either (1) both will be better off or (2) one will be better off and the other no less well off. We do not attempt to judge the justice, or lack of it, in the distribution of welfare be-

contains a family of indifference curves, and in which the X axis shows alternative units of policy X and the Y axis shows alternative units of policy Y. Each point on an indifference curve, we now know, represents a combination of X and Y, as, for purposes of illustration, better police protection and fewer graft-taking politicians respectively. We also know that all points on the same indifference curve represent all the combinations of policies X and Y toward which the individual is indifferent—he feels as well off with one combination as with any other on the same curve. The reader will also recall our comments concerning the shape of indifference curves: They are drawn so that they flow toward and away from the zero intercept so that some curves are farther from the zero intercept than are others. This is an important consideration in the analysis. Consider a movement along the downward slope of curve 1 in Figure 1-9.

Figure 1-9.

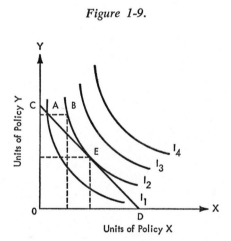

The movement, obviously, involves a substitution of X for Y. Now suppose we invoke the principle of diminishing marginal rate of substitution. As the individual demands more of policy X for policy Y, he obtains more X and therefore the relative utility of X declines. He also obtains less of policy Y, thus increasing the relative utility of Y. As a result, he has to secure more and more of X for given units of Y to obtain the same degree of satisfaction. This is why, as we have explained, indifference curves are shaped as they are. Now if we assume that people prefer more of a value to less of it, then indifference curves farther from point 0 will represent more preferred situations than those closer to 0. Compare points A and B in Figure 1-9. Since B represents the same amount of policy Y but more of policy X, it follows that B is on a higher indifference curve than A. The political problem for any member of the polity is to find an indifference curve that is within his resources and is, at the same time, on the highest indifference curve that he can get to, given his resource constraints. *This explains the low level of political participation among the deprived segments of the population.*

A useful way of thinking about personal resources and political participation is to conceive of society as extending from a central point to a peripheral point with those closest to the center possessing the greater political resources and, hence, characterized by higher levels of political participation. The usefulness of this conception, referred to as the Center-Periphery Dimension, derives from the fact that it involves considerably more than SES (socioeconomic status), which is normally regarded as composed of education, income, and occupation.[13] We show the dimension in Table 1-2 because of its possible application in testing rather precisely the conclusions that flow from our use of indifference analysis.

TABLE 1-2

The Center-Periphery Dimension

Center		Periphery
+	SES	—
+	Length of residence	—
+	Amount of group activity	—
+	Urban-rural residence	—
+	Integration into community	—
+	Sense of "centrality"	—
+	Position in communication nets	—
High political resources		Low political resources

If an individual has only a vote, or if he finds it difficult to vote because he is low on one or more of the relevant indices shown in Table 1-2, as, for instance, position in communication nets, he will demand less of any set of policies than will those with higher levels of personal resources. This point may be shown as follows: Suppose that the costs of two policies mentioned earlier (concerning police protection and bribe-taking politicians) are given in the polity—in the short run it is not possible to haggle over the costs of the policies. Now, given an individual's resources and the cost of policy X, an individual can secure a certain amount of X (e.g., better policy protection) shown by point D in Figure 1-9. Similarly, he can secure relief from corrupt politicians, as shown by the point C. Or he may choose to secure a combination of policies. The line CD shows all possible combinations of X and Y that he can secure, given his resources. The combination

[13] See Milbrath, *op. cit.,* pp. 111–113.

he will actually secure will be point E; since it is the tangency point between his resource line and the indifference curve, it is the highest indifference curve he can get to while still remaining within his resources. Since all policies cost something, he has arrived at his most preferred position given his social resources. This, we would argue, explains the political "apathy" of the underclass, or those on the edge of the Center-Periphery Dimension, rather than any insensitivity to their own fate.[14] Our use of indifference analysis leads us to expect the poor to suffer more from inadequate police protection and from corrupt politicians than those with larger resource bases. This is apparently the case. The virtue of this sort of analysis is that it does not provide *ad hoc* explanations but enables one to arrive, in the manner just shown, at real propositions that may be tested empirically.

The indifference curve technique may also be used to illustrate how an alteration in the availability of a public policy affects the extent to which a policy-seeker will change his behavior with respect to that policy or to other policies. Any alteration in the availability of a policy involves two consequences: they are referred to in economics as the income and the substitution effects. The income effect in politics may be referred to as the "political resource" effect (or "resource" effect) simply because we include more than money as a social resource. We may show the effect as follows. Assume political actor A, who is characterized by a given social position (and hence a given set of political resources), and who finds, for whatever reason, that a policy which interests him has become available at less than previously established cost. The result, clearly, is that A now has more actual political resources than previously. Of course, a decrease in the availability of a policy would reduce his resources. Now, one of the things we know most certainly about political behavior, as we have just mentioned, is that social position correlates closely with political behavior. For example, rich men act more politically than poor men. We have just shown that this fact is predictable from indifference analysis. In short, a decrease or an increase in the availability of a policy will affect any individual's orientation to that policy. The *extent* of this change in behavior is what we mean by the political resource effect. Figure 1-10 shows this effect graphically. The figure shows the resource line CD. A reduction in the cost of policy X means that individual A can get now more of X, say OF, which is tangent to a new and higher indifference curve I_2, at point M. The *total* effect, then, of the reduced cost of policy X is a shift from the combination of policies represented by the point E to that represented by the point M,

[14] Contrast this analysis with Joseph Schumpeter's statement that ". . . the typical citizen drops down to a lower level of mental performance as soon as he enters the political field. . . . He becomes a primitive again" (*Capitalism, Socialism, and Democracy* [New York: Harper & Brothers, 1947], pp. 261–262).

a shift equivalent to an increase in personal resources. In order to show the increase in resources apart from the alteration in the price of policy X, we have to show what amount of resources would enable individual A to secure the new indifference level. Consider that at the old cost of policy X, but at the new resource level implied by the shift from CD to HJ, individual A would demand a policy bundle at point K. One can now observe and distinguish the two consequences in the alteration of the cost of policy X.

Figure 1-10.

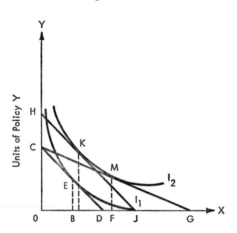

What we have called the political resource effect is shown by the shift from E to K. What we have earlier explained as the substitution effect involves a further shift from K to M. We might call this substitution effect in politics the "policy-alteration" shift.[15]

Let us be clear about what we are saying: *If* the cost of policy X had not changed, but *if* actor A's income had increased to a new level, he would change his political behavior from a demand for policy bundle E to policy bundle K. But with his new resource base the *relative* cost of policies have changed. As a result, at point K the political market's rate of policy-alteration is not the same as actor A's preferred policy alteration. Actor A would thus demand more X than Y, that is, more police protection and less freedom from corrupt politicians, until point M, representing a particular constellation of X and Y, is reached.

One other important observation to be made here is that an alteration, in this case a decrease, in the price of policy X led to a greater demand for more of *both* X and Y. Let us briefly examine the meaning of this fact. It would suggest, for example, that any public policy designed to assist any individual or group will have consequences that the policy-makers may not anticipate. Public education extended to all citizens reduces the cost of education for those who could not otherwise achieve it; the *real* resources of those individuals are increased and more education is demanded—just as the great expansion in higher public education demonstrates. But also more of other things will be simultaneously demanded. The policy alteration effect would produce new combinations of political demands, and changes would result in the character of decisions, and decision-makers, in the polity.

Typically, then, a reduction in the cost of a policy will lead to an increase in quantity demand of the policy—as in the case of demands for education or public health programs. But this is not always the case. In some instances, the reduced cost of a policy will lead to a decline in the quantity of a policy demanded. This seeming paradox would obtain with respect to public policies designed for the underdogs in society—a political concept approximately analogous to the economists' "inferior goods." Consider any of the welfare programs of the government as they form any substantial portion of an individual's resource base. If welfare programs become "cheaper," that is, greater in magnitude and availability, the individual's resource base might be increased to such a point that he would prefer less of the inferior policy; he would employ his now greater resources to secure a superior policy, say government employment, vocational retraining, transportation out of a depressed area, better schools, or whatever.[16] This is very likely the case, although it is a point that the politicians have yet to grasp securely.

Now let us consider another important and related problem. We know from Figure 1-10 that if an individual has resource level CD, he will demand quantity B of policy X, and that if his real resource base increases to CG he will demand quantity M of policy X. That is, we have two points on a policy indifference curve. But one cannot yet say with any certainty what sorts of policy combinations would be preferred at any resource line less than CD, intermediate to CD and CG, or greater than CG. However, we can deal with this problem by considering any alternative cost of policy X, drawing in any appropriate resource lines from point C to the abscissa and obtain as many points as one might wish. Connecting the points thus derived would result in a policy demand curve for any individual, given his resource base. Now, of course, actor A is not the only person interested in better police protection or relief from corrupt politicians. Indeed, there is a political market in which these policies are sought, and we are logically

---

[16] For references, see Raymond W. Mack, *Social Mobility: Thirty Years of Research and Theory* (Syracuse: Syracuse University Press, 1957).

concerned with the total, or aggregate, demand for these policies, for example, the total social demand for better police protection. The problem is a simple one: If all individual demands are known, the total demand may be secured simply by adding the level of police protection at a given cost desired by all individuals in the market. By doing this at all alternative costs that interest us, we obtain the policy demand curve for the whole society, or any portion of the society that is of interest. In Chapter III, we will show why one might want to do this.

A Note on Time, Intensity, and Terms of Exchange in Isolated Bargaining

With respect to exchange, one must also be concerned to know something about the *length* of the bargaining period prior to exchange decisions (the time factor) and about the *intensity* factor in exchange. To illustrate the impact of these two elements in an exchange decision, we may focus upon an isolated bargaining situation and use certain economic ideas to examine how time and intensity (and the *terms* of exchange) get involved in an exchange decision.

Isolated bargaining ". . . occurs between two parties who must either trade with each other or not at all."[17] Two elements to isolated bargaining are the terms on which the bargain is contracted and the distribution of the bargaining gains between the trading partners. Neoclassical international trade theory includes an analytical concept useful in explaining postulates regarding these aspects of isolated bargaining. We refer to the Marshall-Edgeworth offer curve, which has long been employed in conceptualizing both the terms on which international trade is conducted and the manner by which the trade gains are distributed between trading partners.[18] Marshall-Edgeworth offer curves, as employed here, present unique insights into the problems of conflict resolution and the function of intensity in a bargaining situation. We can begin by making two assumptions: (1) As a bargaining period draws to a close, each partner will offer its partner progressively more favorable terms of trade to assure that some beneficial bargain will be contracted; (2) the trading partner whose reciprocal demand is relatively more intense, other things being equal, will enjoy the more favorable terms of trade. Several other assumptions are useful. They are: (3) two bargain-

[17] Tiber Scitovsky, *Welfare and Competition* (Homewood, Ill.: Richard D. Irwin, 1958), p. 5.

[18] An excellent book by Charles P. Kindleberger, *International Economics* (Homewood, Ill.: Richard D. Irwin, 1959), Chapters 6–8, provides a comprehensive treatment of international trade theory, including the Marshall-Edgeworth Offer Curve technique introduced here.

ing entities exist; (4) two bargaining rewards, X and Y, exist; (5) bargaining is conducted to determine a mutually acceptable ratio at which X and Y are exchanged; (6) entity A controls the supply of reward X and B controls Y; (7) costs of obtaining X and Y are identical for entities A and B; (8) a given pattern of demand intensity for each bargainer is fixed for the bargaining period; and (9) each person is unaware of the other's demand intensity. The abscissa in Figure 1-11 measures units of good Y from the zero intercept to some positive quantity. Offer curve OC_A portrays the ratios at which entity A is willing to offer good X to entity B in exchange for Y. It shows that as time increases, and the bargaining period draws to a close, entity A is willing to offer more X for a unit of Y. The offer curve OC_A shows that entity A is willing to exchange a unit of X for 3 units of Y early in the bargaining period (subperiod 1 in Table 1-3), but gradually becomes willing to offer relatively more units of X per unit of Y, or conversely, to accept relatively less of Y per unit of X. At some point, A is willing to offer its good at an exchange ratio of $1X : 1Y$ (subperiod 5, Table 1-3). OC_B portrays the ratios at which entity B is willing to exchange good Y to entity A for good X. Entity B is presumed to behave similarly to A. Early in the bargaining period, B is willing to exchange a unit of Y for 3 units of X (subperiod 1 in Table 1-3), but, as time passes, B becomes willing to accept fewer units of X per unit of Y. Entity B is also willing to exchange at the ratio of $1Y : 1X$ (in subperiod 5, Table 1-3). We assume that the bargaining period is composed of six subperiods. At the end of each subperiod, the institutional structure permits each entity to make explicit the ratio at which

Figure 1-11.

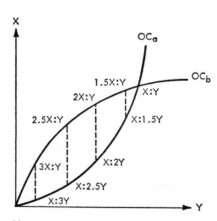

Note: Offer curves of trading partners A and B are based on data given in Table 1-3.

it is prepared to exchange. We have done this to assure that the equilibrium exchange ratio of $1X : 1Y$ is acceptable to each trading partner at the same time, in this case after subperiod 5. Table 1-3 shows the acceptable exchange ratios for A and B at the end of each subperiod.

TABLE 1-3

Acceptable Exchange Ratios

Subperiod	A's Ratio	B's Ratio
1	$X : 3Y$	$3X : Y$
2	$X : 2.5Y$	$2.5X : Y$
3	$X : 2Y$	$2X : Y$
4	$X : 1.5Y$	$1.5X : Y$
5	$X : 1Y$	$1X : Y$
6	$X : .8Y$	$.5X : Y$

In Figure 1-12 we assume that A's offer curve is modified by a change in its intensity of demand for good X. The new offer curve OC_A indicates that after subperiod 1, for example, entity A is willing to give up 1.5 units of X for every 3 units of Y. Entity A is now prepared to exchange relatively more units of X for Y because the latter good is demanded relatively more intensely than originally was the case. After subperiod 2, entity A is willing to exchange at a ratio of $2.5X : Y$, a ratio that entity B also finds acceptable after that subperiod. Table 1-4 shows the acceptable exchange ratios at the end of each bargaining subperiod after entity A's offer curve has been modified.

TABLE 1-4

Acceptable Exchange Ratios

Subperiod	A's Modified Ratio	B's Ratio
1	$1.5X : Y$	$3X : Y$
2	$2.5X : Y$	$2.5X : Y$
3	$3.0X : Y$	$2X : Y$
4	$3.5X : Y$	$1.5X : Y$
5	$4.0X : Y$	$1X : Y$
6	$4.5X : Y$	$.5X : Y$

In Figure 1-8 we noted that an exchange from F to a point on the "contract curve" somewhere between H and G (or along the dotted line) would make both parties better off. That is, both entities A and B would be in more preferred positions. But the relative degree to which they are better off is dependent, at least partially, on their relative intensity or demand for each other's rewards. When A's offer curve shifted from OC_A to OC_A', it meant that A would be willing to accept relatively less advantageous terms of trade. This enabled B to achieve a position less close to H. The converse

Figure 1-12.

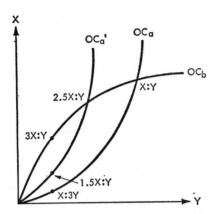

Note: Offer curves of trading partners A and B
are based on data given in Table 1-4.

would be true if the pattern were reversed and B were the entity whose offer curve shifted and reflected a more intensive demand on his part.

We can now interpret our use of Marshall-Edgeworth offer curves as follows: The relatively more intense the reciprocal demand of the trading entities for each other's good, the more probable it is that a mutually acceptable exchange will be contracted and the more probable it is that the bargain will be contracted early in the bargaining period. We may also conclude that a key bargaining tactic is for an entity to encourage its trading partner to demand its good relatively more intensely to ensure (a) that some bargain is more probable, and (b) that, given this bargain, more favorable terms of exchange will be contracted.[19]

In conclusion, we have thus far attempted to do the following: (a) to argue that exchange is likely to be mutually beneficial to trading partners whether in economy or polity; (b) to use cardinal utility analysis as a point of departure in developing decision-making principles guiding the behavior of reasonably prudent and rational actors; (c) to develop ordinal utility analysis, basically the indifference technique, as our central means of outlining those principles; (d) to use the so-called "box diagram" in Figure 1-8 to deal with two actors rationally conducting an exchange; (e) to introduce the important concepts of time and intensity in an exchange process,

[19] Offer curves are not translated into indifference curves, but if reference is made to Figure 1-8 with the above argument in mind, it will be clear that if individual B's demand is relatively less intense than A's, and if he is less concerned to bargain, the equilibrium point on the contract curve will show B in a relatively more preferred position than A, other things being equal (refer to the above assumptions).

specifically that of isolated bargaining; and (f) to discuss, on an introductory basis, political exchange, focusing on one individual's role in the exchange. We now turn to our development of political exchange in general equilibrium.

TWO

---

*Exchange in General
Political Equilibrium*

The result of abandoning, for the most part, the idea that satisfactions can be added means that indifference curve analysis of the behavior of a rational individual has taken the place of the Marshallian type of analysis. The assumption that the individual tries to maximize his satisfaction is retained, although to maximize satisfaction no longer means achieving the largest sum total of satisfaction, but rather reaching the most preferred possible position. An individual can say that he is higher up a hill, or lower down a hill, or at the same height, but, unlike ordinary numbers, such estimates are not marked in feet, or units of satisfaction. In other words, they are ordinal numbers, that is, first, second, and third estimates or, as in the case of an individual on a hill, judgments as to the contour line of the hill upon which the individual stands. There is no question of adding up these numbers; an individual cannot add ordinal numbers. It does not matter whether they are labeled one, two, three, or one, two, four. They could just as well be labeled by any other set of numbers. All that matters is that a higher contour, representing in some circumstances greater satisfaction, must have a higher number than a lower contour.

31

Let us re-emphasize this important point within the framework of the present chapter: Assume a situation in which there are only two goods, X and Y, and let us focus our attention on some one individual. As far as economic things are concerned, his satisfaction now depends only on the amounts of X and Y he can consume. (We could just as easily think of policy-seekers choosing between alternative public policies.) The next step is to draw contour lines on a graph, the two coordinates of which represent amounts of X and Y. As we have emphasized several times, any two points on one such contour line thus represent collections of goods toward which an individual is indifferent. In order to draw a contour line, take a given collection of goods, represented by a point A on the graph, and then discover, by asking the individual, all the other collections of X and Y such that he says he is indifferent toward each of these collections B, C, D, and E, and collection A. It is then assumed that he is indifferent toward B and C, C and D, and so on. In other words, it is assumed that indifference is a *transitive* relation.[1] This means that if a person is indifferent toward A and B, and toward B and C, then he must be indifferent toward A and C. Thus, indifference curves are actually contour lines and may be determined as we have described. It should now be clear what is meant when we say that, in our analysis, satisfactions need not (cannot) be added. Given all of this, we may now make certain additional assumptions, which we will apply later, concerning the individuals in a political system.

(1) They prefer a larger collection of goods or policies to a smaller one. (2) If they once choose any collection rather than another of goods or policies they will always do so. (3) Their choices are transitive. (4) Any chosen collection of utilities should be chosen in only one cost-resource situation, that is, any change in relative costs will always cause some change in what is obtained.

Given these assumptions, a consistent set of behavior lines can be composed, such that if an individual reaches a point that lies above the curve belonging to the point from which he started, then he has secured a collection of utilities that is higher on the order of his choices than the previous collection. And this will be the criterion that we shall use to say that any individual is better off than before. The fulfillment of this criterion may, of course, be taken, by anyone who wishes to do so, to imply that the

---

[1] The notion of transitivity has been examined both by economists and sociologists. While there is some disagreement on the validity of the transitivity assumption as it relates to individual choice, we believe it to be a useful one. We would argue (1) that the assumption is valid, and (2) that it is related directly to the degree to which one preferred position is greater than the previously attained position. That is, the more preferred one position is over another, the more plausible the assumption of transitivity. The interested reader is referred to an excellent survey of this matter in Arnold A. Weinstein, "Individual Preference Intransitivity," *Southern Economic Journal*, XXXIV (January 1968), pp. 335–343.

person is more satisfied. As I. M. D. Little points out ". . . it does not follow logically from the meaning of behavior (contour or indifference) lines that anyone who can be said to be on 'a higher behavior line' must also be said to have more satisfaction—all that follows is that he is in a chosen position. This conclusion may not sound very novel. Indeed, many people have probably thought that the indifference curve analysis was about choices, and not about satisfactions. But so long as the concept 'indifference' was retained and not defined in terms of choice, a rigorous interpretation in such terms was impossible."[2]

With the foregoing in mind, the specific theoretical task in this chapter is to develop a general adumbration of political exchange relationships of such an order that insight into the central logic of politics is enhanced.[3] The terms we will use here have the precise meanings ascribed to them in Chapter I. The exchange processes analyzed here are heuristic and, as well, simplistic in the sense that they concern a limited number of variables. The processes have serious implications for change, although they retain certain of the static qualities of neo-orthodox economic theory. As it stands, the formulation can be tested at certain points by obvious data (as illustrated in Chapter I); data can be brought to bear in the testing of non-obvious hypotheses logically derived from the model. Certain of the variables selected for analysis here and in subsequent chapters have been taken from the theoretical contributions of Dahl and Lindblom, Buchanan and Tullock, Riker, Downs, and Schattschneider.[4] Others have not heretofore been applied in political analysis. The body of theory upon which much of the model is based is not limited to these theorists, but includes the whole

[2] I. M. D. Little, *Critique of Welfare Economics* (London: Oxford University Press, 1958), pp. 26–37.

[3] We do not deny that there are aspects to politics other than simply the efforts by individuals to maximize their gains from exchanges. For example, maintenance of the exchange process itself may be more important to a given individual than any single exchange. Thus, if an exchange will endanger the perpetuation of the process of exchange, it may not be made even though it would maximize someone's short-run interest. With respect to this issue, which goes to the question of political constitutions, see James M. Buchanan and Gordon Tullock, *The Calculus of Consent* (Ann Arbor: University of Michigan Press, 1962). Analyses of the several objectives of the business firm in which profit maximization is only one goal can be found in William J. Baumol, *Business Behavior, Value and Growth* (New York: The Macmillan Co., 1959); Richard M. Cyert and James G. March, *A Behavioral Theory of the Firm* (Englewood Cliffs, N.J.: Prentice-Hall, 1963); R. Marris, *The Economic Theory of Managerial Capitalism* (New York: The Free Press of Glencoe, 1964).

[4] Robert A. Dahl and Charles E. Lindblom, *Politics, Economics, and Welfare* (New York: Harper & Brothers, 1953); Buchanan and Tullock, *op. cit.;* William Riker, *The Theory of Political Coalitions* (New Haven: Yale University Press, 1962); Anthony Downs, *An Economic Theory of Democracy* (New York: Harper and Brothers, 1957); E. E. Schattschneider, *The Semi-Sovereign People* (New York: Holt, Rinehart and Winston, 1960).

tradition of positive theory-building in formal economics including, in particular, indifference analysis.

Mitchell has recently argued that ". . . political processes involving bargaining, coalition-formation, competition, and the analysis of constitutional rules and public policies . . ." are problems than can usefully be understood through the application of axiomatic models derived from economic theory.[5] Several of these processes are confronted here in a general fashion through the application of various such pedagogical techniques. Before articulating the elements of the processes, an explanatory comment must be inserted.

The purpose of this chapter is to describe some fundamental and representative processes (fundamental in the sense that they are either basic to the actual operation of polities or constitute bench-marks against which deviations can be measured) which are temporarily assumed to work in the polity. However, certain of the stipulations which we shall introduce are not *fully* descriptive of the actual operation of any particular political system. We deliberately abstract only in order to clarify, to clear away the underbrush so that, in some sense, we have a better idea of what seems to be going on in politics. Some of the stipulations, then, are stronger or more realistic than others, but, in all cases, they will hopefully assist in outlining one way to think about basic political processes. For example, we will stipulate that political resources are widely (we will not say equitably) distributed and that entry into interest groups is unrestrained. Of course, some people have very few resources, and not all groups welcome new members. But we will, for the moment, make such assumptions anyway, because we will then have an evaluative gauge to employ in Chapters IV and V when we examine political structures that do not have such properties and rules and, as we argue in Chapter VI, are more realistic.[6]

[5] William C. Mitchell, *Sociological Analysis and Politics* (Englewood Cliffs, N.J.: Prentice-Hall, 1967), p. 192.

[6] As Abraham Kaplan notes, science is never a matter of taking ". . . 'note of all the facts.' . . . We work . . . at some level of abstraction, and to abstract from certain factors is nothing other than to ignore them. The contemporary theory of games is startling in its generality and power precisely because its abstract formulations bypass so much of the complexity of the rules and play which, *as players*, we have become accustomed to regarding as the significant features of the game; but it remains true that these features are unimportant for the solution of the problems which the theory poses" (*The Conduct of Inquiry* [San Francisco: Chandler, 1964], p. 166). With respect to the new political economy, the same point is made somewhat differently in William C. Mitchell, "The Shape of Political Theory to Come: From Political Sociology to Political Economy," *American Behavioral Scientist*, XI (November–December 1967), pp. 19–20, and, by implication, by David Braybrooke, "An Illustrative Miniature Axiomatic System," in Nelson W. Polsby, Robert A. Dentler, and Paul A. Smith (eds.), *Politics and Society* (Boston: Houghton Mifflin, 1963), pp. 119–130.

In his *Sociological Analysis and Politics,* Mitchell points out that the concept of "exchange" is important because it focuses upon "interaction" and not just interdependence.[7] Too, the non-zero sum character of certain political exchanges, as Tullock and Buchanan have shown, adds another dimension to a social process often viewed solely in terms of power and authority.[8] In part, the following discussion can be viewed as an elaborate definition of political exchange. More concisely, we may define political exchanges as those consisting in the mutual flows of costs and rewards between and among political actors. Exchange will occur, we assume, when it is to the mutual advantage of the actors to trade costs for rewards (i.e., when rewards outweigh costs as those factors relate to the subjective preference functions of the actors).

How may exchange be assumed to work in the polity? That is the question we are now concerned to answer.

THE SYSTEM: ITS STRUCTURE

The political exchange that we suggest here is conducted within the context of a "market structure" containing three variable sets: the political system's decision-making *rules* (the constitution); the system's *properties;* and the *actors* within the system. A system is defined, for our purposes, simply and nonrigorously, as the ". . . coordinated activities of two or more persons (actors)."[9] The system discussed here is one in which the actors, some of whom are members of interest groups, are in interpersonal, intergroup, and intragroup conflict. Conflict exists when two or more actors maintain opposing interests; paradoxically, however, it is because of conflict that collective action (a generic form of human action of which political action is a part) takes place, and thus makes reasonable the assertion that conflict ". . . strengthens pre-existing ties or contributes to the establishment of unifying ties where none existed before."[10] It may be observed that this definition of a social system does not rely on shared values, a point that is securing greater emphasis in contemporary social research.

SYSTEM RULES

The political system's decision-making, or constitutional, rules consist of the components described below and are to be understood as condition-

---

[7] Mitchell, *op. cit.,* p. 76.

[8] Buchanan and Tullock, *op. cit.*

[9] Robert C. North, Howard E. Koch, Jr. and Dina A. Zinnes, "The Integrative Functions of Conflict," *The Journal of Conflict Resolution,* IV (September 1960), p. 155.

[10] *Ibid.*

ing the sorts of political exchanges that may occur within the polity at the broadest level of conception.[11] As we will state them here, they appear to approach the essential logic of the decision-making rules operative in Anglo-American political systems, even though the necessary deviations and embellishments of the actual rules in such systems are not discussed here.[12] *Rule 1:* Actors are free to enter and to leave political interest groups without restriction. *Rule 2:* Political interest groups are free to form coalitions to conduct bargaining with other groups, or they may bargain independently. *Rule 3:* Bargains between or among political interest groups are contracts defining the allocation of rewards and costs incurred in the bargain. *Rule 4:* Political interest groups are free to form coalitions in order to compete to affect the authoritative allocation of rewards and costs by the government. *Rule 5:* Governmental allocations are contracts defining rewards and costs. *Rule 6:* Actors are free to enter the political process through which the government is selected. We assume for the moment that no extraconstitutional force impedes the operation of these rules.

It should be emphasized that, although the rules make possible the admission of actors into interest groups, we are not advancing an interest-group theory of politics, but rather a theory in which such groups play a part. The rules and properties do not require group membership for any particular individual, and, indeed, we assume (know) that large numbers of actors may well choose not to participate in group activity. But we are less interested in this question now than in the question of political exchange.

SYSTEM PROCESSES

Definitions of two basic processes are required, and the definitions we will use coincide with those generally accepted in economic theory. Iso-

---

[11] Buchanan and Tullock, *op. cit.,* gives greatest attention to the development of a strict economic theory of political constitutions. The rules posited here are taken as givens for the moment, and we do not treat the matter of their formation.

[12] Gabriel A. Almond, "Comparative Political Systems," *The Journal of Politics,* 18 (August 1956), pp. 391–404. Such systems are ". . . homogeneous, secular. . . . The political system is saturated with the atmosphere of the market. Groups of electors come to the political market with votes to sell in exchange for policies. Holders of office in the formal-legal role structure tend to be viewed as agents and instrumentalities, or as brokers occupying points in the bargaining process. . . . It takes on the atmosphere of a game" (p. 398). Actually, this activity is often more of a ritual than a game, a point made in what should be required reading for game theorists, Claude Lévi-Strauss, *The Savage Mind* (Chicago: University of Chicago Press, 1966), pp. 30–32.

lated bargaining is defined as conduct between or among groups to establish an exchange contract defining the allocation of rewards and costs between or among themselves. This occurs between or among parties who must exchange with each other or not at all. Isolated bargaining, thus, is similar to collective bargaining between a firm and a labor union, an exchange that determines the allocation of gains and losses between the bargainers and does not normally directly involve the government or the participation of some other outside party. (Of course, by establishing Rules 1, 2, 3, and 4, the government participates indirectly.) We have discussed some of the properties of isolated bargaining in the previous chapter. Competitive bargaining is defined as conduct between or among groups to affect the authoritative allocation of rewards and costs, as determined by governmental decision, when the government has a series of alternative distributions from which to choose.[13] As used here, then, competition refers to a situation involving, say, two entities competing against each other to affect a specific allocation of resources (such as locating a federal project in Area A or Area B) by the government, where it is free to choose A or B, in which one competitor receives all resources given.

We refer to isolated bargaining simply as *bargaining,* and competitive bargaining as *competition.*

SYSTEM PROPERTIES

Having outlined the rules and processes of the political system, we must now necessarily stipulate the crucial characteristics, or properties, of the actor's preferences and the distribution and control of resources and information within the system. Again, the properties stipulated have a fundamental similarity to Anglo-American systems; the static qualities of certain properties, however, are temporarily necessary to permit the analysis to proceed. The system is characterized by the following properties: *Property 1:* Preferences to maximize individual rewards and to minimize individual costs are given and fixed for each actor. *Property 2:* Each actor prefers the system's constitution to any alternative set of rules, and he accepts the system's allocation of rewards and costs. *Property 3:* Resources are controlled by individuals and by the government and are fixed in quantity, quality, and distribution. We conceive of system resources, of course, as not limited to physical or economic resources but as including psychological

---

[13] These concepts are more fully explained, in terms of their usage in orthodox economic theory, by Tiber Scitovsky, *Welfare and Competition* (Homewood, Ill.: Richard D. Irwin, 1958), p. 12.

and social resources as well.[14] *Property 4:* Information and technical knowledge are fixed and given in the system.[15] *Property 5:* Resources, information, and technology are *relatively* decentralized in their distribution throughout the system.[16]

[14] The term *resources* refers here to any value amenable to exchange, and could be conceptualized variously. A useful taxonomy would be Harold D. Lasswell and Abraham Kaplan's politically relevant welfare values (health and safety, wealth, skill, enlightenment) and deference values (power, respect, rectitude, affection) (*Power and Society* [New Haven: Yale University Press, 1950], pp. 55–56). In terms of Parsonian systems analysis, the relevant exchange variables would consist of variables entering the polity from other social sectors (control of productivity, commitment of services, interest demands, political supports, legitimation of authority, legality of powers of office) and variables leaving the polity (opportunity for effectiveness, allocation and fluid resources, policy decisions, leadership responsibility, operative responsibility, moral responsibilities for collective interest). These relationships are delineated and explained in Mitchell, *op. cit.,* pp. 78–81, 83. The input-output categories of David Easton, *A Systems Analysis of Political Life* (New York: John Wiley & Sons, 1965) and Gabriel A. Almond, "A Developmental Approach to Political Systems," *World Politics,* XVII (January 1965), pp. 183–214, are also relevant. In addition, time is a political value of great importance, although it is rarely studied by political scientists. An empirical study of social exchange is reported by Peter Blau, *The Dynamics of Bureaucracy* (Chicago: University of Chicago Press, 1955), p. 108, which involved a consultative process in a public bureaucracy in which enlightenment and skill were the variables of exchange.

[15] Downs, *op. cit.,* pp. 207–276 and Chapter 14, has dealt rigorously with the question of information and the political process. Most pertinent is Downs's observation that information costs often make nonparticipation rational. It should be emphasized that we do not assume that information is equitably distributed. Indeed, it seems clear that political actors behave in the absence of information which, if available, would restructure their preference functions. In fact, Kant believed that perpetual peace would be the consequence of perfect information possessed by self-interested people. On the state of public information, see Robert E. Lane and David O. Sears, *Public Opinion* (Englewood Cliffs, N.J.: Prentice-Hall, 1964); V. O. Key, Jr., *Public Opinion and American Democracy* (New York: Alfred A. Knopf, 1961); and Angus Campbell, Philip E. Converse, Warren Miller, and Donald E. Stokes, *The American Voter* (New York: John Wiley & Sons, 1960). In spite of such information restraints, V. O. Key reintroduced the notion of intelligent participation in a brilliant and important study in which he argued that voters do respond to political issues in a rational fashion (*The Responsible Electorate: Rationality in Presidential Voting, 1936–1960* [Cambridge: Harvard University Press, 1966]). For support for Key's thesis, see Harry Daudt, *Floating Voters and the Floating Vote* (Leiden: H. E. Stenfert Kroese, N.V., 1961), especially Chapter 16.

[16] Relatively decentralized is not the same as equitably decentralized. On the distribution of resources in the United States, there tends to be two major views, represented by group theorists on the one hand and by elite theorists on the other. The problem is an empirical one, and our concern in this book is to show how *either* system would manage its political exchanges. We deal with these questions in Chapters IV and V. For contending views on the distribution of resources in America, see C. Wright Mills, *The Power Elite* (New York: Oxford University Press, 1956), and a reply by Arnold M. Rose, *The Power Structure* (New York: Oxford University Press, 1967).

System Actors

Within the constraints of the rules and the properties of the system, four sets of actors engage in relationships involving political exchange. All of these sets, with the exception of the set of politicians, are what we have heretofore called policy-seekers; but each group seeks policies in different ways. Politicians, of course, are the policy-makers. At this point the four sets of actors and their attributes are simply posited (a more detailed description of their activities follows shortly). The terms given to the sets of actors are not ours but are taken from the literature and have been adopted because, in our view, they give greater precision than do alternative terms in describing the functions and relationships of political actors. The four types of actors are: *Type 1*—beneficiary members of interest groups;[17] *Type 2*—fiduciary members of interest groups;[18] *Type 3*—politicians (who compose the government); *Type 4*—spectators within the audience.[19]

In addition, each actor is assumed to be rational in the limited sense that each actor will try to improve his political position; that is, each actor, when given at least two alternative courses of action with differing outcomes in terms of rewards and costs, will choose that alternative leading to the larger welfare.[20] Each actor performs a function within the system,

[17] Riker, *op. cit.*, pp. 24–25.

[18] *Ibid.* We assume that "the" beneficiary is a representative one; that is, his preferences are representative of all the other beneficiaries in the group. Also, we are aware that it is difficult to conceive of one fiduciary acting for each group. It is obvious that groups differ in size and complexity. The larger and more complex a group is, the more likely it is that there will be an organizational structure consisting of many individuals interacting (exchanging *within* the organization) so as to produce decisions concerning which goals and tactics to pursue. We do not attempt to deal with the question of the formation of consensus within the group; we simply conceive of "the" fiduciary as the ultimate decision-maker in the group (even though he is aided and influenced by others). For a most interesting, and somewhat alternative, view of these matters, see Mancur Olson, Jr., *The Logic of Collective Action* (Cambridge, Mass.: Harvard University Press, 1965), Chapters 1 and 2, *passim,* and especially the discussions of group size, rationality, and coercion.

[19] Schattschneider, *op. cit.*, pp. 16–22 and *passim*. The term "spectator" is used in Schattschneider's sense to refer to the impact upon the outcome of a conflict of those not closely involved in any single issue: "The spectators are an integral part of the situation for, as likely as not, the *audience* determines the outcome of a flight" (p. 2). We would qualify this statement by suggesting that it is an empirical question as to how many conflicts, and to what degree, will be decided by the audience, although we will speculate later with respect to this question.

[20] Although we assume rationality as defined, we also stipulate, with Buchanan and Tullock, that "in analyzing the behavior of the individual in the political process, there is an important element of uncertainty present that cannot be left out of account. . . . In the case of any specific decision rule for

and the role structure within the system is given and fixed. The political system, then, is composed of four sets of rational actors who maximize (in the sense previously defined) net welfare. Welfare for each actor is subjectively derived and is based upon the actors' subjective preference-orderings, which establish certain varieties of political consequences toward which the individual is indifferent or that range from the most to the least preferred. Below we formally state how the system may be assumed to operate; later chapters will add to the analysis presented here, and will point up the dynamic character of political exchange. We hasten to say that the "model" outlined below is only one of many possible formulations that could serve to generate insights into political exchange. All we really want to do is to raise simple but central processes to the level of consciousness.

THE BENEFICIARY

The beneficiary is an actor who is a member of one or more groups. His role within the system is to establish demand priorities that maximize his individual welfare. His welfare is derived from the excess value of rewards over costs successfully demanded from the system through group membership. His membership in any group is dependent upon three determinants: (1) the possession of resources required for group membership; (2) the knowledge of rewards and costs associated with membership in any group; and (3) as stipulated by the rules, the existence of nonrestraints against group membership. A beneficiary may be a member of a number of groups each involved in an issue in which he has an interest.

Beneficiary *rewards* from group membership may be viewed twofold: (1) the beneficiary receives those resources allocated to his interest through group bargaining; and (2) he receives those resources allocated to his interest through competition. The *costs* involved in securing such benefits are also twofold: (1) the costs incurred in gathering the information necessary to determine his costs and rewards from various groups; and (2) membership costs, which are contributions of resources to the group fiduciary. We assume that, due to the decentralized distribution of resources, no beneficiary possesses the resources required to bargain or compete individually. The beneficiary maximizes his welfare by allocating

---

the group, the individual participant has no way of knowing the final outcome, the social choice, at the time he makes his own contribution to the outcome. This problem is overcome in part by realizing that decision-making is a continuous activity . . . each decision representing only one link in a long-time chain of social action" *op. cit.,* p. 37.

his scarce resources among groups as follows (although he may choose only one group):

Figure 2-1.

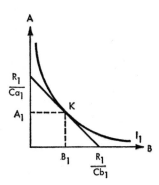

In this manner, the individual beneficiary attains the most chosen position possible. He allocates A_1 of his relatively scarce resources R_1 to group A, and B_1 of these resources to group B, given the membership costs of Ca_1 and Cb_1. He can obtain the position K on indifference curve I_1, but cannot choose a position more specific than somewhere along I_1. Each beneficiary shares in the groups' reward in a manner proportional to the group resources he chooses to contribute.

THE FIDUCIARY

The fiduciary is a political actor who represents beneficiaries as a group agent. His role within the system is to bargain with other group fiduciaries on issues in which his beneficiaries have an interest and to compete with other group fiduciaries to affect the authoritative allocation of resources by the government on issues interesting his beneficiaries.

The fiduciary derives his welfare from the excess of the value of resources which beneficiaries contribute to the group over the resource costs he incurs in bargaining and competing with other beneficiaries. To maximize the value of his welfare, the fiduciary must allocate resources efficiently so as, first, to satisfy the demands of the beneficiaries who support him, and, second, to conserve a portion of these resources as his own reward. The personal costs which the fiduciary pays are the expenditures of skill, time, and energy resources required in the bargaining and competitive process.

The fiduciary first selects a set of issues the outcomes of which affect the welfare of the group beneficiaries. He must decide to employ one or both of two strategies—either to bargain with other fiduciaries on issues or to compete with them for the authoritative allocation of resources by the government. The fiduciary chooses to bargain with other fiduciaries if the interests of the fiduciaries in the two groups are not mutually exclusive and if "sharing" is possible. He chooses to compete with other fiduciaries if the interests of the beneficiaries are mutually exclusive and if sharing is not possible. In later sections, we shall be most concerned with the problem of competition, or those social conflicts that involve the government directly.

The fiduciary is free to form coalitions with other groups in bargaining and competition, and will do so when it is efficient, or when the value of coalition cost is less than the reward value received through coalescing.[21] The rewards and costs of bargaining and competition are divisible between or among groups when they coalesce on an issue, and their distribution is a matter of contract. The distribution of costs and rewards is made in a twofold manner: first, on the basis of the group beneficiaries' ability to contribute resources to pay the costs of coalition formation and decision-making. The group with the greater resources receives the greater reward based on differences in resources endowment. And second, the allocation is made on the basis of the group's intensity of demand. When the intensities are dissimilar, though not so great as to preclude coalition formation, the group less intensely demanding the particular reward on any issue receives the greater reward. The group demanding the reward more intensely is willing to accept a lesser proportion of rewards and contribute a larger proportion of costs than the group more indifferent toward the reward. This process was analyzed in Chapter I. When the fiduciary has selected his issues, his bargaining, and/or his competitive strategy, and has determined whether or not to coalesce on an issue, he allocates scarce resources to maximize the total welfare of the group as follows:

[21] Very little work has been done, as William Riker has recently noted, to *verify* theories of rational coalition formation ("Bargaining in a Three-Person Game," *American Political Science Review,* LXI [September 1967], p. 642). For exceptions, see this article by Riker, as well as L. E. Fouraker, "Level of Aspiration in Group Decision Making," in S. Messick and A. H. Broyfield (eds.), *Decisions and Choice* (New York: McGraw-Hill, 1964); William A. Gamson, "An Experimental Test of a Theory of Coalition Formation," *American Sociological Review,* XXVI (August 1961), pp. 565–573; Anatol Rapoport and Albert M. Chammah, *Prisoners' Dilemma* (Ann Arbor: University of Michigan Press, 1965); and Thomas Schelling, *The Strategy of Conflict* (Cambridge: Harvard University Press, 1960). It is not clear what these quite small-scale studies will contribute to the understanding of massive social processes, although they do tend to confirm our postulates of rationality and the importance of rules in the making of decisions.

Figure 2-2.

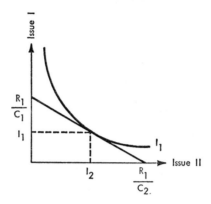

He allocates I_1 of the resources contributed by beneficiaries to Issue I_1 and I_2 to Issue *II*. The total disposable resources are R_I, and the costs of bargaining or competing on the issues are C_1 and C_2 respectively.

The exchange is an understood contract between the beneficiaries and the fiduciary. Each fiduciary is willing to accept the exchange because he has most efficiently used his skill. The limitation to his skill is his ability to bargain, to compete, and to choose correctly those issues on which to coalesce; because of this limitation he is unable to gain more rewards for beneficiaries, and consequently to contract for more resources (rewards). In an equilibrium state, no fiduciary is inclined to leave one group and to enter another. By doing so, he would accept a lower reward and, consequently, not maximize his welfare, either through a less efficient use of his particular skills (an increase in cost), or through his ability to attain fewer rewards for beneficiaries. (We assume, for example, that the skills of a labor leader would be less efficiently used in an alternative role.)

Before turning our attention to the other actors in our system, we believe examination of Figure 2-3 is helpful in understanding certain key points that we have attempted to make. Assume that *Oa* and *Ob* are group beneficiaries, and that *X* and *Y* are the rewards from group membership. We know that groups bargain by exchanging units of *X* and *Y*, and that such exchanges affect the interests of beneficiaries. We assume that indifference curves *Ia* and *Ia₁* are so-called "community indifference curves" for all the beneficiaries in Group A, and *Ib*, and *Ib₁* are community indifference curves for all beneficiaries in Group B. In the sense in which we are using them, the community indifference curves are aggregates of individual indifference curves for the beneficiaries involved. If one group has some combination of greater resources, less intense reciprocal demand, and relatively more skillful fiduciaries, it will attain the relatively more preferred position somewhere between points G and F on the contract curve.

We might also suppose that Oa and Ob are two beneficiaries in the *same* group with indifference curves Ia, Ia_1, Ib, and Ib_1 respectively. The beneficiary with some combination of greater amount of resources to contribute, and a relatively less intensive demand for combinations of X and Y, will attain the relatively more preferred position somewhere along the contract curve between points H and G.

And we might still further suppose that Oa and Ob are fiduciaries wishing to attain most preferred positions in terms of the resources accrued to them as residual payments for their bargaining skills. The rewards may be thought of in terms of goods X and Y to be attained with the accrued resources. The fiduciary with some combination of greater bargaining skill and greater quantitative and/or qualitative resource endowment transferred to him by his group's beneficiaries will attain the relatively more

Figure 2-3.

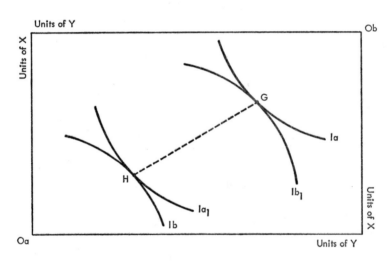

preferred position on the contract curve somewhere between points H and G.

THE SPECTATOR

Thus far we have delineated exchanges between beneficiaries and fiduciaries affecting allocations of gains and losses. By assumption the resources throughout the system were decentrally allocated. In other formulations, of course, resources are not allocated in this fashion but are concentrated in ownership or control. This is true for virtually all elite theory and constitutes the conventional point of departure between pluralist and elitist theories. Although our assumptions are *temporarily* in the pluralist tradition and provide for decentralized resource allocations, the problem is essentially an empirical one, and, as we demonstrate below, neither tradition is essentially incompatible with our approach, given the implications for change implicit in the exchange concept.

Each spectator is defined as an actor who is a member of no group—either because he is interested in no issue, or because he perceives that the value of rewards from group membership is less than the value of membership costs. The spectator is not, then, a beneficiary, because he has exercised rational choice in the sense previously defined. While he possesses information and resources of some order or magnitude, he does not employ them because he calculates that it is not in his interest to do so. He is willing to accept the *external effects* from system decisions made by other individuals.

However, the spectator is not a passive member of the political system; the function of the spectators is to assist in the selection of the government. All actors within the system elect the government by majority vote in any election. The spectators account for a significant proportion of the vote and, consequently, affect strongly the outcome of an election. The outcome of an election determines the allocation of gains and losses in two ways: First, the authoritative allocation of resources through government action on issues is affected. Second, the determination is made whether or not to keep the political system's decision-making rules and properties intact. Decision-making rules and properties regulate coalitions between and among groups and bargaining between or among them; the consequence of these rules and properties includes an impact on the allocation of certain social costs and rewards flowing from group bargaining. Allocation of rewards and costs through bargaining and competition has external effects on individual spectators.

In his exchanges with the polity, the individual spectator receives rewards and bears costs as do all other actors in the system. The rewards that each spectator receives are *external rewards* that result from competition and bargaining. An example of an external reward would be the lower price a spectator pays when a tariff has been reduced because of the activities of fiduciaries representing large business firms who want domestic tariff reductions for a reciprocal reduction in foreign tariffs. Each spectator also bears *external costs* arising from these processes, for example, in the form of taxes or prices. The so-called "white backlash" may also be understood in these terms: The result of the backlash may be a state government staffed with politicians who, the spectators believe, will control a situation that they fear for whatever reasons. The result rewards beneficiaries and fiduciaries holding similar attitudes, for example, realtor associations. It will penalize "losing" spectators as well as beneficiaries and fiduciaries not holding these attitudes, for example, civil rights groups.

Further costs are measured by the resources each spectator must transfer to the government for its authoritative allocation. In an equilibrium state, x number of spectators voting in an election is an important determinant of the outcome. The spectators, then, indirectly reward the beneficiaries and fiduciaries whose interests most closely coincide with the interests of the majority of x spectators by the election of a government that will allocate rewards and costs in a manner consistent with the interests of those beneficiaries and fiduciaries.

The spectator does not vote on a single issue but rather on a set of issues in an election. Consequently, he may favor politician or party A on some issues and B on others. He will vote for the politician or party that he calculates will maximize his total reward on all issues over total costs on all issues. It may be that for certain spectators net welfare is negative, but so long as such spectators remain a minority they will not be able, other things being equal, to alter the system's rules, properties, or its allocation of rewards and costs. Of course, they (as well as other losing minorities) may seek, perhaps successfully, violent or extraconstitutional action to overthrow the existing structural pattern of exchange relationships.

For the most part, then, each spectator participates in a political process in which his "vote" gives assent to a process whereby he receives rewards primarily through (1) direct benefits from some "public goods" supplied by politicians, (2) external benefits from some "private goods" supplied to beneficiaries by fiduciaries, and (3) external benefits from some "public goods" supplied to beneficiaries by politicians through the urging of fiduciaries. This highlights, we believe, the difficulty inherent in establishing a dichotomy between private or public goods. The "vote" of each spectator also gives assent to a process whereby he gives up resources (1) directly through public allocations of costs, such as taxes or military conscription, or (2) indirectly through private allocations of costs, such as health problems associated with using certain "consumer" goods or breathing city air polluted by private individuals or institutions. The spectator may accept the ratio of his benefits to his costs and, therefore, be apolitical, or political only in the sense that he votes. Again, he may not accept the ratio and turn his support to competing politicians. Or he may also attempt to become more political by trying to enter political markets either as a new fiduciary or as a new politician. Or he may become a potential radical reformer. Or, finally, he may drop out of the system altogether when he chooses not to accept his benefit to cost ratio and finds that *all* political markets have been closed to him by the existing political markets' structural barriers. Even the revolutionary markets offer no attraction and no benefits.

THE POLITICIAN

The politician is an actor who participates in the process of government, that is, in the authoritative allocation of rewards and costs for a whole society. His role is to make decisions on issues about which groups and their fiduciaries compete and which indirectly affect the spectators. His rewards are twofold: first, the power, prestige, and deference gained from his role in the allocative process; and second, the resources he gets from two sources—the taxes paid by all actors (some of which are diverted to salaries and perquisites of office) and the contributions he receives from fiduciaries (for campaigns and, from time to time, for bribes). His costs are the time, energy, and campaign contributions spent in being elected and in authoritatively allocating resources and costs.

The politician participates in two exchange sets: the first with all voters,[22] especially spectators, and the second with fiduciaries of groups. He must make allocative decisions to meet with the approval of enough spectators in order to remain in office. Should he not do so, spectators undertake the cost of changing politicians and elect to office those aspirants who will allocate resources in a manner spectators will accept. The politician who correctly perceives the spectators' interests, and who satisfies them most efficiently, receives power by being elected to office. The politician, however, must also conduct an exchange with each fiduciary. Each fiduciary elects to compete on certain issues in which the interests of group beneficiaries are involved. The fiduciary allocates the scarce resources he commands to politicians on these issues.

The politicians are initially restrained by spectators in elections and within this restraint they decide exchanges that favor those groups who transfer the greater amount of resources to politicians at election time. The politician receives these resources from fiduciaries in return for a specific authoritative allocation of community resources, for example, taxes. Since fiduciaries have efficiently allocated resources in the competitive process, each group's gains are maximized and losses minimized on each issue.

The resource contributions from fiduciaries to politicians enable the latter group to influence the ranking of priorities by the spectators who elect them to office. That is, politicians attempt to affect the degree to which spectators accept the distribution of rewards and costs acceptable to ben-

[22] As modified, in the manner proposed by Downs, *op. cit.*

eficiaries, as determined by group fiduciaries' bargaining and competition, and which results in welfare for politicians.

COMPETING POLITICIANS

The competing politician is an actor in the polity who conspires to displace the politicians in power and to assume authoritative public office thereby. His role is to offer the electorate changes in the existing distribution of costs and benefits among spectators, beneficiaries, and fiduciaries in an effort to convince the electorate to elect him to office.

Competing politicians receive gains in the form of resources donated by losing fiduciaries (that is, those fiduciaries whose welfare would be maximized through a change in politicians). Losses are incurred in the process of expending contributions from fiduciaries and personal resources in an effort to persuade the electorate to support competing politicians. Until and unless he is successful in achieving office, the competing politician suffers a net loss of welfare.

The exchanges that exist in the polity as discussed above may be summarized in Table 2-1. There are many other sorts of political exchanges, of course, but, as we understand it, the ones cited above may be conceived as the broadest, most representative, and most basic exchanges that occur. They might, therefore, be referred to as fundamental political exchange processes.

IMPLICATIONS FOR CHANGE

In economic theory, change in any market of exchanges is ordinarily studied through the technique of comparative static analysis. A change in any determinant of the system's state (rules, properties, individual preferences) can be analyzed deductively to indicate probable effects within the system as a whole, offering the advantage of assisting in the location of the proximate variable(s) that, for whatever reason, is (are) *producing* change, and, more importantly, it assists in analyzing the *effects* of change.

For example, a change in the electorate's choice of a government might produce new politicians in office who would undertake to alter the properties of the system in order to achieve a new distribution of costs and values and to strengthen their appeal to the electorate thereby. Too, change in the system's rules and properties, which condition the existing structure of exchange patterns, may well be altered in a revolutionary situation in which existing rules and properties do not facilitate the processes of "acceptable" exchange. Again, as an example, it may occur that the spectators do not accept the existing distribution of values and costs, nor any distribu-

TABLE 2-1

Representative Exchanges in the Polity

Actors	Rewards	Costs
Beneficiaries	Resources allocated to priorities demanded by group fiduciaries through bargaining and competition	Resources to group as membership fees, e.g., decision-making resources
Fiduciaries	Residual of resources distributed by beneficiaries over resource costs in bargaining and competition	Time, energy, and skill spent in bargaining and competition
Spectators	External benefits indirectly received from authoritative allocation of rewards by government, or external benefits from group bargaining decisions	External community resource costs through taxation, prices, etc., due to authoritative governmental allocations and the results of group bargaining
Politicians	Power and prestige associated with authority to allocate rewards and costs plus opportunities to extract private utility from taxes, bribes, and other payments	Time, energy, and skill spent in campaigning and authoritatively allocating rewards and costs

tion offered by competing politicians and, therefore, are willing to undertake the cost of revolutionary change because off-setting expected returns from an alternative system: they feel that they have little to lose but possibly much to gain.

Other things being equal, the polity would tend to move toward some equilibrium state (which simply means a state in which no incentive to exchange exists that would alter current patterns). However, the existence of a measure of uncertainty in the polity, combined with the possibility of new information or other resources being introduced into the system, would be consistent with the emergence of new sets of individual preferences and, consequently, new sets of demands. Some of these factors are taken up in the following chapter.

Again, we point out that there are many other exchanges that occur in politics. In Chapter III, for example, we will discuss one such smaller and less obvious market that involves important public bureaucrats and aspirants to bureaucratic power.

THREE

Exchange in Partial Equilibrium:
The Market for
Administrative Elites

A change in an individual's political resources, or in relative costs, affects his demand for rewards. This is a point that we have mentioned several times. His response to a change in cost shows a certain regularity. We know that in most cases the individual's quantity demand for a reward increases when its cost falls, and falls when its cost rises. This would not necessarily be true, however, as we showed earlier, for policies such as public welfare—a despised "inferior" policy. We know also that these behavior patterns are deducible from an individual's indifference map.

We can draw this phenomenon into a demand curve, which shows how an individual's quantity demand for a reward is affected by changes in reward cost.[1] When his resource endowment is fixed (R_1), and cost changes (from a_1 to a_2), the individual market opportunities can be repre-

[1] Tiber Scitovsky, *Welfare and Competition* (Homewood, Ill.: Richard D. Irwin, 1958), Chapter 13; and Leftwich, *op. cit.*, pp. 77–82.

sented graphically by a demand curve (or schedule). By connecting all points of tangency between political resource lines and indifference curves, we can derive the individual's political demand schedule. This is shown in Figure 3-1.

As drawn in Figure 3-1, the demand curve shows that the lower the cost of A (i.e., $Ca_2 < Ca_1$) the greater the individual's demand for A ($Qa_1 > Qa_2$). This relation between cost and the individual's demand can be shown more graphically by transferring the cost consumption curve ($\bar{c}$) from the indifference map of Figure 3-1 onto the cost quantity diagram of Figure 3-2 (Da). Here the horizontal axis measures the quantity of A as before, but the vertical axis shows the cost of A: The cost-consumption curve on Figure 3-1 is an individual's demand curve with a downward slope. This demand curve corresponds to the relationship between cost and the individual's demand for policies.

The advantage of representing the individual's response to a change in policy costs with the aid of the demand curve is that such individual demand curves can be added together to form a demand curve for any political market. To perform this addition, all the policy-seekers in a market must face the same general cost. In this case the market demand curve is obtained by adding, for each ordinate (cost), the abscissae of the individual demand curves of all the policy-seekers in the market (i.e., the quantity demanded by each individual at that cost). This is the horizontal addition of the curves of all individuals.

Figure 3-1.

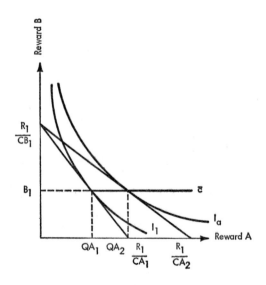

Figure 3-2.

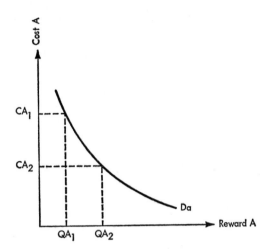

These concepts are useful in analyzing exchange markets such as those that involve administrative and potential administrative elites. They permit the analysis to take place by focusing upon the structural characteristics of demand and supply, a focus basic to most of the remainder of our analysis.

In this section we isolate one political market and show how it might be understood within the framework of the analysis thus far developed; we will now deal primarily with market equilibrium—the kind of equilibrium that can frequently be observed in political markets. Now in politics, just as in the economy, there are many exchange markets. In Chapters IV and V, we will be concerned with various ways in which political exchange markets may be *structured,* by which we refer to the number of people in a market, how many of them are policy-seekers, how many policy-makers, and so forth. Differences in the structures of political markets are important because they tell us a great deal about the exchanges that may occur within them. There are also what we might call substantive markets, or markets that refer to exchange relationships in politics that most people know about but have really not considered in exchange terms. It would be a Herculean task to mention all of the markets that occur to us and, indeed, the political system is so complex that many substantive markets, even important ones, would escape observation. For this reason it is often better to focus concern on the structure of political markets; if one is interested, then, in a particular substantive market, he might analyze it by first discovering its structure. To analyze something is to "break it down" into as many pieces as are convenient so that an understanding of how the pieces work together (or fail to work together) makes it possible to understand the whole thing. In the discussion below, we have arbitrarily (although it is intrinsically interesting to us) selected a substantive market, and we have broken it down to get a better understanding of it. Other exchange markets could be similarly analyzed; thus, our purpose here is only *illustrative* of how substantive exchange markets may be analyzed. Of course, an analysis cannot proceed willy-nilly. It has to follow certain rules, and the rules we follow are axiomatic and are derived from the discussions of Chapters I and II. Axiomatic reasoning proceeds from reasonable assumptions to testable propositions and, if it proceeds correctly, is preferable to other forms of analysis because its explanations are suggested before, rather than after, an empirical examination of the facts of the matter. An axiomatic theory may, of course, be wrong, just as *ad hoc* theories may be wrong, but when elements of axiomatic theories are wrong, the parts that make up the total theory may be corrected and the theory thus made a better one.

Substantive political exchange markets would, we suggest, be very large in number. Representative markets would include ". . . elections, referendums, or plebiscites, . . ." or markets in which ". . . candidates and governments offer policies and abilities in exchange for support or votes."[2] Other markets are organized around other political institutions: judicial markets (in which there are trade-offs of public support or "legitimacy" for particular decisions, or trade-offs of "liberty" for "order");[3] districting markets (in which political assemblies trade off districts and regions that have varying political propensities);[4] ethnic markets (in which a Negro is appointed to the Supreme Court for ethnic support, or in which the "ticket" is balanced ethnically for the same reason).[5] Of course, the terms of trade may be ambiguous, but this is an analytical, not a social problem. In fact, Gouldner's analysis leads us to search for the reasons

[2] William C. Mitchell, *Sociological Analysis and Politics* (Englewood Cliffs, N.J.: Prentice-Hall, 1967), p. 85.

[3] Several studies of the courts are particularly instructive if read from a perspective that emphasizes exchange. See, for example, John Schmidhauser, *The Supreme Court: Its Politics, Personalities and Procedures* (New York: Holt, Rinehart & Winston, 1960); Walter T. Murphy, *Elements of Judicial Strategy* (Chicago: University of Chicago Press, 1964); Richard A. Watson, Rondal G. Downing, and Fredrick C. Spiegal, "Bar Politics, Judicial Selection and the Representation of Social Interests," *American Political Science Review,* LXI (March 1967), pp. 54–71.

[4] The "Great Compromise" of 1787 is a well-known example in American history in which union was traded for power. The "deal" of 1876 is also instructive — the Republicans handed over politics in the South to the planters ("Democrats") in return for a sympathetic position on economic issues.

[5] On the persistence of ethnicity in politics, see Raymond E. Wolfinger, "The Development and Persistence of Ethnic Voting," *American Political Science Review,* LIV (December 1965), pp. 896–908; Michael Parenti, "Ethnic Politics and the Persistence of Ethnic Identification," *American Political Science Review,* LXI (September 1967), pp. 717–727.

why the terms of exchange are often ambiguous; he suggests that the ambiguity is functional by (1) projecting obligations into the future (thus producing stability in the interim), and (2) by, over long periods, making it unclear who is in whose debt (thus decreasing demands and increasing the perceived obligations of all parties to the exchange).[6]

The substantive political market we have selected to analyze for illustrative purposes is a market that is of increasing social importance and concerns the process whereby individuals are recruited into elite roles in the public bureaucracy. We encourage others to analyze the many alternative substantive exchange markets since, in our view, this is the next great field for theoretical advance in political science.[7]

Specifically, our concern is to analyze the nonmonetary exchange market within which the recruitment of administrative elites is conducted. Our purpose is not only to explore the possible use of concepts from economics that we have introduced in analyzing the process of elite recruitment, but it is also to select and relate functionally, and in a logical fashion, the most relevant variables involved in the process.

Development of the analysis proceeds in two parts. In the first part a relatively uncompounded and static equilibrium formulation is advanced. It is modified in the second part of this chapter and made more complex, more realistic, and less static.

THE LESS COMPLEX MARKET

The nonmonetary administrative elite recruitment market brings together two groups of individuals in order to effect an exchange. The elite recruitment group is composed of individuals who are assumed motivated to acquire decision-making power within the administrative process of government by occupying authoritative administrative offices. We may think of these people as aspiring policy-makers. The established elite group is composed of individuals who hold authoritative office and who are assumed to be motivated to hire the skills of elite recruits. We may think of these people as policy-makers. An exchange of *rewards* is effected when an elite recruit exchanges his skills for an administrative elite appointment. In the exchange process, individuals within each group are assumed also to incur a nonmonetary *cost*. Each elite recruit incurs the cost of acquiring

---

[6] Alvin W. Gouldner, "The Norm of Reciprocity: A Preliminary Statement," *American Sociological Review,* XXV (April 1960), p. 161.

[7] Two volumes have appeared recently that deal with the analysis of bureaucracies from the viewpoint of the new political economy: Anthony Downs, *Inside Bureaucracy* (Boston: Little, Brown, 1967), and Gordon Tullock, *The Politics of Bureaucracy* (Washington, D.C.: Public Affairs Press, 1965). It may be that public administration will be the first of political science's traditional areas to be fully explored with this approach.

the skills which he exchanges for an administrative appointment. Further, each established administrative elite incurs the cost of exchanging a portion of his decision-making in order to acquire the skills of the recruit. Thus, power and skill are the elements of exchange in this market.[8]

Figure 3-3 illustrates the conditions under which, and the degree to which, exchange is undertaken in the nonmonetary recruitment market. The figure illustrates three important schedules determined by the motivations of the individuals within the group. The functions do not refer to an individual but rather to the aggregate of all individuals within the group.

The ordinate in Figure 3-3 measures the alternate units of non-monetary costs a recruit must incur in order to acquire alternative levels of skill useful in administration. Cost (or skill) is measured from zero to some positive level (OC). The cost unit is assumed to be the time and effort required to gain skill either through experience, a formal education, or both. The abscissa measures the number of administrative appointments from zero to some positive level (OA). Each appointment is assumed to involve equal increments of decision-making power (i.e., the ability to make authoritative allocations of rewards and costs in society).

The three important schedules within the model are as follows: (1) the demand schedule for appointments by the elite recruit group; (2) the supply, or offer, schedule of appointments by the established elite group;[9] and (3) the reservation demand schedule for appointments by the established elite group.[10] The demand schedule (D_oD_o) shows the number of elite recruits who demand administrative elite appointments at each cost level of acquiring skills useful in administration. The level of cost, the independent variable, determines the quantity of appointments demanded, the dependent variable, at each cost level. At a relatively high level of cost

---

[8] "Skill" refers, of course, to control of a constellation of characteristics more extensive than simple competence in technical bureaucratic activities, although certainly these are included. The "higher" administrative skills have to do with the staging of administrative performances, insight into the essentially political nature of bureaucracy, talent in the manipulation of symbols and organizational loyalty. For a seminal study of staging (and, implicitly, exchange) see Erving Goffman, *The Presentation of Self in Everyday Life* (New York: Doubleday, 1959); on organizations as power systems, see Robert Presthus, *The Organizational Society* (New York: Vintage Books, 1965), especially Chapter 6, and Tullock, *op. cit.;* and, for a most important study of organizations as symbols, see Murray Edelman, *The Symbolic Uses of Politics* (Urbana: University of Illinois Press, 1964), particularly Chapters 2 and 3.

[9] Our discussion of supply and demand analysis and the notion of equilibrium is roughly comparable to the treatment such concepts receive in most texts on economic principles, such as Paul A. Samuelson, *Economics* (7th ed.; New York: McGraw-Hill, 1967), Chapter 4.

[10] For a discussion of what is meant by reservation demand, see George J. Stigler, *The Theory of Price* (New York: The Macmillan Co., 1966), pp. 96–98. Stigler's remarks are in terms of storeable goods but are relevant to our point.

(and consequently high level of skill), fewer individuals are prepared to incur the cost than at lower cost levels. As the costs decrease, more individuals demand such appointments because more individuals are presumed willing to undertake the cost. The demand for administrative elite appointments, then, is inversely related to the cost of acquiring skills required for such appointments.

Determinants of the demand schedule are presumed to be known, and their values are assumed to remain constant. The determinants are: (1) monetary costs required to acquire skill; (2) the belief system of each individual in terms of the values of organizational participation, for example, income, status, power, congeniality, and opportunities for achievement;[11] and (3) alternative employment opportunities available to the elite recruits in industry and the nonmonetary rewards associated with such employment. We can now state the first basic assumption.

Basic Assumption 1: Given the values of determinants of demand, the demand schedule shows the quantity of elite appointments demanded at each cost level of acquiring skills useful in administration.

The supply schedule (S_oS_o) relates the number of administrative appointments that the established elite group is prepared to offer at each alternative level of skill (or cost). The level of skill as the independent variable determines the quantity of administrative elite appointments offered by the established elite group, the dependent variable. At a relatively high level of skill, the established elite group is prepared to offer a greater quantity of appointments than at lower levels of skill. The supply of administrative elite appointments is positively related to the level of skill, or the cost of acquiring skill, to fulfill such appointments.

The determinants of the supply schedule are assumed to be known and their values are assumed to remain constant. The determinants are: (1) the degree of societal complexity and the resulting heightened role differentiation demands more competent specialists in order to conduct the administrative process efficiently; and (2) demands from the government

---

[11] The assumptions concerning the values to be derived from organizations are consonant with other analyses. On status, see C. Wright Mills, *White Collar* (New York: Oxford University Press, 1951), p. 243; H. Wilensky, *Intellectuals in Trade Unions* (Glencoe, Ill.: The Free Press, 1956), p. 146; Dwain Marvick, *Career Perspectives in a Bureaucratic Setting* (Ann Arbor: University of Michigan Press, 1954), pp. 52–54; on achievement, see David McClelland, *The Achieving Society* (Princeton, N.J.: Van Nostrand, 1961); on power, see Robert Presthus, *Behavioral Approaches to Public Administration* (University, Ala.: University of Alabama Press, 1965), pp. 103–136; on income, see Daniel Bell, *Work and Its Discontents* (Boston: Beacon, 1956), p. 29; on congeniality, see Franklin Kilpatrick, Milton C. Cummings, and M. Kent Jennings, *The Image of the Federal Service* (Washington, D.C.: The Brookings Institution, 1964), pp. 83–85.

for an administrative process that is effective in producing an "output" that the government's constituency requires.[12] We can state the following basic assumption.

> *Basic Assumption 2: Given the value of the determinants of supply, the supply schedule shows the quantity of administrative elite appointments offered at each level of skill useful in administration.*

The formulation also contains a reservation demand schedule for administrative elite appointments by the established elite group. It is actually a modified supply (or offer) schedule.[13] The reservation demand schedule $(T_o T_o)$ indicates the absolute quantity of elite appointments that the established administrative elite group is prepared to offer. It is presumed that this level of administrative elite appointments will not be exceeded. First, assume that not all individuals employed within the organization are elites. There is a category of individuals who are employed by elites and who do not affect the authoritative allocation of rewards and costs throughout the society. Assume also that the determinants of the reservation demand function are twofold. First, assume that the total resource power of administrative elites (command over the allocation of resources to system goals) is limited because the government allocates limited resources to administrative organizations (designated as $\bar{P}$). Second, assume that a portion of the resources must be used in the recruitment process $(r\bar{P})$. Third, assume that the established elite group is reluctant to share its power to allocate authoritatively (P) resources and that it reserves the power to allocate some proportion of the resources $(s\bar{P})$. The reservation demand for allocative power limits the absolute quantity of appointments to $(T_o T_o)$. The reservation demand schedule, or the modified supply schedule, is $T_o = f[P - (r\bar{P} + s\bar{P})]$. We can state the following basic assumption.

---

[12] Both supply determinants are consistent with the propositions of many modern organizational theories. The value of efficiency as an organizational goal has been classically stated by Herbert A. Simon, Donald W. Smithburg, and Victor A. Thompson, *Public Administration* (New York: Alfred A. Knopf, 1959), pp. 17–18 and *passim*. The government's interest in the output of administrative agencies and the satisfactions of clientele groups have been observed by many writers, among them David B. Truman, *The Governmental Process* (New York: Alfred A. Knopf, 1955), pp. 439–446; Earl Latham, *The Group Basis of Politics* (Ithaca, N.Y.: Cornell University Press, 1952), Chapter 1; Marver Bernstein, *Regulating Business by Independent Commissions* (Princeton: Princeton University Press, 1955), Chapter 3.

[13] Reservation demand functions in bureaucracies have received, as far as we know, no systematic treatments. However, the ubiquitous existence of hierarchy in organizations is itself evidence that such a function might well be postulated. Typically, power is commensurate with hierarchy, which, in turn, implies the limited availability of power positions. See Robert K. Merton, *Social Theory and Social Structure* (rev. ed.; Glencoe, Ill.: The Free Press, 1957), p. 195.

Basic Assumption 3: There is some quantity of administrative elite appointments that the established elite group is not prepared to exceed regardless of the level of skill acquired by the elite recruit group and this quantity may be more or less than the equilibrium quantity of appointments.

Figure 3-3.

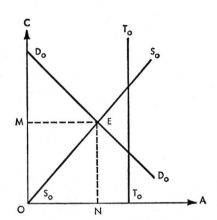

E:	intersection of supply and demand functions at equilibrium
OC:	alternative levels of cost
OA:	alternative quantities of administrative elite appointments
D_0D_0:	demand function for elite appointments by elite recruit group
S_0S_0:	supply (offer) function for elite appointments by established administrative elite group
T_0T_0:	reservation demand function for elite appointments by established elite group
OM:	equilibrium level of cost (or skill)
ON:	equilibrium level of appointments to administrative process

In Figure 3-3, there is one equilibrium level of cost (skill) that equates the quantity of administrative elite appointments demanded with the quantity of appointments offered by the established elite. At cost (skill) level *OM*, a total of *ON* appointments are demanded and offered. At no other level of cost (or skill) is this true. At levels of cost (or skill) less than *OM*, there is an excess demand for appointments. At the level of *OS*, for example, in Figure 3-4, there is an excess demand for appointments *OP* to *OQ*. At this level more individuals are prepared to incur the cost than there are appointments offered. The excess demand causes elite recruits to compete against each other in order to attain a higher level of skill needed to gain an appointment. Competition among elite recruits causes the cost to increase because people are prepared to invest more time and effort to acquire a higher skill level. However, certain individuals are not prepared to undertake the cost required to improve their marketability and, therefore, drop out of the market, and quantity demanded shifts back to ON. As the elite recruits compete and increase both cost and skill, the increase in the level of skill means that more appointments are offered by the established elite. The supply, or offer, of appointments increases to ON. The equilibrium level of cost (or skill) and the appointments have once again been attained because forces within the market have operated automatically to restore the original equilibrium.

At any level of cost (or skill) in excess of OM, there is a surplus of appointments. At cost OR, competition among established elites tends to

Figure 3-4.

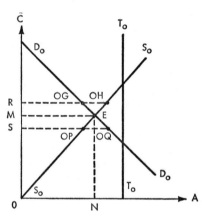

E:	intersection of supply and demand functions at equilibrium
OC:	alternative levels of cost
OA:	alternative quantities of administrative elite appointments
D_oD_o	demand function for elite appointments by elite recruit group
S_oS_o:	supply function for elite appointments by established elite group
T_oT_o:	reservation demand function for elite appointments by established elite group
OM:	equilibrium level of cost (or skill)
ON:	equilibrium level of appointments to administrative process
OG to OH:	surplus of appointments at cost (or skill) level OR
OP to OQ:	deficit of appointments at cost (or skill) level OS

force down the level of cost (or skill) to *OM*—they are now bidding for the services of elite recruits who, at *OM,* demand fewer appointments than established elites are prepared to offer. The established elites compete among themselves and offer appointments at lower levels of skill (or cost). At the lower cost (or skill) level, more individuals enter the elite recruit group because more individuals are prepared to incur the lower cost. When cost drops to *OM,* once again the demand for appointments is equated with the quantity of appointments offered. At *OM,* elite recruits demand, and established elites offer, quantity *ON.* The equilibrium is attained at intersection *E,* independent of exogenous forces. Such a solution is stable in isolation and established elites do not choose to reserve any portion of appointments *ON.* We can state the following basic assumption.

> *Basic Assumption 4: The market determines an equilibrium solution at a skill or cost level at which the quantity of appointments demanded is equal to the quantity of appointments offered or supplied.*

Endogenous forces within the market operate to restore equilibrium automatically. Given the demand, supply, and reservation demand schedules in Figure 3-4, only one equilibrium is possible, and it is at intersection *E.* It is an equilibrium that is stable in isolation. It requires the intervention of no exogenous force to restore equilibrium. It is this type of static equilibrium that has often been justly criticized.[14] However, such criticisms do not obviate the use of a more realistic and less static equilibrium concept. The following section is an effort to construct a market model that is not stable in isolation and that challenges the persistence of the institution of the market within which elite recruitment takes place.

THE MORE COMPLEX MARKET

The first part of this chapter was characterized by a set of *ceteris paribus* conditions in which the values of all supply and demand determinants were assumed known and assumed constant. These assumptions are obviously oversimplified and not completely realistic. For example, it is more likely that the values of such determinants are constantly in a process of change. The method that will be used here to account for such change is comparative static analysis, a notion that was introduced in the last chapter. A change in a determinant's value can be analyzed deductively to indicate probable effects within the market. Assume first, that the monetary cost of acquiring skills useful in administration decreases due to an increase

---

[14] For example, by David Easton, "Limits of the Equilibrium Model in Social Research," in Heinz Eulau, Samuel Eldersveld, and Morris Janowitz (eds.), *Political Behavior* (Glencoe, Ill.: The Free Press, 1956), pp. 397–404.

in the quantity and distribution of economic resources. The entire demand schedule shifts to the right as shown in Figure 3-5. The new demand schedule (D_1D_1) indicates that at each level of cost more individuals are able to enter the elite recruitment group, and consequently a greater quantity of appointments is demanded at each cost level. Monetary restrictions limit fewer individuals from entering the market as members of the recruit group, and, consequently, more individuals demand administrative elite appointments at each level of cost.

Assume further that there has been a change in the value of one deter-

Figure 3-5.

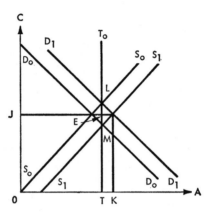

OC:	alternative levels of cost
OA:	alternative quantities of administrative elite appointments
D_0D_0:	demand function for elite appointments by elite recruit group
D_1D_1:	new demand function for elite appointments by elite recruit group after a change in certain determinants of demand
S_0S_0:	supply function for elite appointments by established elite group
S_1S_1:	new supply function for elite appointments by established elite group after a change in certain determinants of supply
T_0T_0:	reservation demand function for elite appointments by established elite group
OJ:	new equilibrium level of cost (or skill)
OK:	potential equilibrium level of administrative appointments
OT:	quantity of administrative appointments offered within the restraint of reservation demand
L:	skill (or cost) level· desired by established elite group at OT
M:	skill (or cost) level desired by elite recruit group at OT

minant of the supply schedule, such as the increasingly complex problems associated with industrial society, causing it to shift to the right to (S_1S_1). This means that the established elite requires a greater quantity of elite recruits at each alternative level of skill (or cost). As Figure 3-5 indicates, there is a reservation demand function (T_oT_o) for administrative appointments by the established elite group; thus, no quantity of appointments in excess of OT are offered. At the *potential* equilibrium solution OJ, the equilibrium level of appointments demanded is OK. At cost (or skill) level OJ, there is a conflict between the two groups that is impossible to resolve through bargaining. On the assumption that the established elite group is powerful enough to limit appointments to OT, the bargaining is conducted to determine the cost (or skill) level. The established elite bargains for a high skill level (point L), and the elite recruit bargains for a lower level (point M). Equal bargaining power by each organized group would approach the solution at point G, and unequal power would benefit the powerful relatively more than the less powerful. Regardless of the outcome of the bargain for a skill (cost) level agreement, no efficient market solution can take place unless the quantity of elite appointment offered increases to OK. A level of appointments less than OK means that societal demands are frustrated because OK appointments are required to satisfy efficiently demands expanded due to increasing societal complexities.

Rather than show a market equilibrium stable in isolation, we have now, based upon reasonable assumptions, shown a situation in which two groups are the center of a conflict that challenges the institutional structure through which elite recruitment takes place. The conflict arises because of the impossibility of the elite recruitment market to effect an efficient equilibrium solution, and this places stress on the market. To perform the administrative process efficiently and to produce an output of administrative services efficiently, the established elite requires the services of OK elite recruits, but only OT are appointed to administrative positions. The market is unstable in isolation and requires intervention from exogenous forces to restore equilibrium and eliminate the institutional stress. Realistically, additional environmental forces, such as governmental pressures, change the outcome of the market. Pressure such as this would regulate the political conflict within the market.

Political conflict, as Schattschneider states, ". . . consists of two parts: (1) the few individuals who are actively engaged at the center and (2) the audience that is irresistibly attracted to the scene. . . . To understand any conflict, it is necessary, therefore, to keep constantly in mind the relations between the combatants and the audience because the audience is likely to do the kind of things that determine the outcome of the [conflict]. This is true because the audience is overwhelming; it is never really neutral; the excitement of the conflict communicates itself to the audience. *This is the basic pattern of all politics.*"[15]

The audience in this case is assumed to be composed of individuals within the society who benefit from an efficient output of administrative services. This makes the audience much more than a passive witness drawn to a conflict—it becomes a participant.

The government, we assume, has ultimate control over the administrative process. Assuming the operation of a systemic feedback process, disruption in administrative efficiency in which the audience (constituency) has an interest is brought to the attention of government. Government is assumed to be the force that intervenes into the conflict within the elite recruitment market. The government intervenes in order to maintain its position by being elected by the audience in the face of the persistent challenges of competitors. Should the government not correctly perceive the feedback, a competitor will do so and displace the existing government by offering the audience an efficient solution. But either the "old" or "new" government is forced to intervene into the elite recruit market.

The government's intervention is an exogenous force to restore an efficient equilibrium solution in the market and is analyzed in Figure 3-6. It is a replica of Figure 3-5 with one important change: The reservation demand function for administrative elite appointments by the established elite has shifted to (T_1T_1) because of the government's intervention. At (T_1T_1) equilibrium quantity of appointments OK is achieved. The number of elite recruits willing to incur the cost level OJ demands precisely the quantity of administrative appointments that are now offered by the established elite at this cost (or skill) level.

However, the new equilibrium is not restored by a reaction of the independent variable to a change in the value of the dependent variable, because the reservation demand schedule is not dependent upon cost. An exogenous variable—the government—intervened and served to coerce an efficient performance from the market and to eliminate the source of stress from the market. The government coerced equilibrium from what Easton calls a "parapolitical system"[16] through its control of the administrative process. A parapolitical system is a subsystem in a societal political system, and the elite recruitment market is such a subsystem. The parapolitical, or market, structure has effects on the society as a whole, and if these effects are unacceptable, the power available to the societal political system will be exercised to control the functioning of the market. The conclusion derived from the foregoing analysis is as follows:

[15] E. E. Schattschneider, *The Semi-Sovereign People* (New York: Holt, Rinehart & Winston, 1960), p. 2.

[16] David Easton, *A Framework for Political Analysis* (Englewood Cliffs, N.J.: Prentice-Hall, 1965), pp. 50–56.

Figure 3-6.

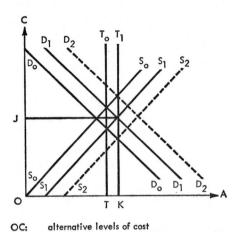

OC: alternative levels of cost
OA: alternative quantities of administrative elite
        appointments
$D_0 D_0$:   demand function for elite appointments by
        elite recruit group
$D_1 D_1$:   new demand function for elite appointments
        by elite recruit group after a change in
        certain determinants of demand
$S_0 S_0$:   supply function of elite appointments by
        established elite group
$S_1 S_1$:   new supply function of elite appointments
        by established elite group after a change in
        certain determinants of supply
$T_0 T_0$:   reservation demand function for elite appoint-
        ments by established elite group
$T_1 T_1$:   new reservation demand function for elite
        appointments by established elite group
        after intervention by the government
OJ: equilibrium level of cost (or skill)
OK: equilibrium level of administrative appoint-
        ments

Conclusion: The government intervenes into the market to coerce an equilibrium quantity of appointments when the reservation demand of the administrative elite group prevents attainment of equilibrium.

The above equilibrium solution is not maintained indefinitely. The demand schedule is assumed to be partially dependent upon the supply and reservation demand schedules. As the established administrative elite group is forced by government to shift its reservation demand function to the right to $(T_1 T_1)$ in order to permit appointments to expand to *OK*, the existing and potential members of the elite recruit group are affected by this change. The expansionary shift in the reservation demand schedule is assumed to be visible to both the elite recruitment group and the audience (constituency). This affects the expectations of potential and existing members of the elite recruit group. This will stimulate the development of programs designed to induce additional individuals into the elite recruitment group. This increases the expectations of individuals within the elite recruit group as well as potentially producing more members of the group. In this manner, a shift in the supply schedule is a partial determinant of demand—it affects the psychological propensities of individuals.

The result is a shift in the aggregate demand schedule further to $(D_2 D_2)$. A shift in the demand schedule to $(D_2 D_2)$ forces a new equilibrium quantity of appointments in excess of OK. But the quantity of OK is the maximum that established elites are prepared to offer. The equilibrium solution at cost OJ and quantity OK are temporary and unstable in isolation over time. Again, there must be intervention into the institutional process by an exogenous force if stress is to be reduced and efficiency maximized.

The reader will now, hopefully, be able to understand the entire structure of our views on political exchange as they have been developed thus far. In the present analysis, we undertook to explain a particular political market through the use of rather simple demand and supply schedules, by explaining how they originate and what they mean. They are transferred from indifference analysis, which is the manner in which we think political exchange can best be expressed and which explains, better than any alternative conception of which we are aware, the terms of exchange and the conditions under which exchange will take place.

ADMINISTRATIVE ELITE RECRUITMENT: AN EXAMPLE

The fate of an elite, Lasswell has written, is bound up with its skill in the process of politics: violence, organization, bargaining, and propaganda.[17] All of these major political variables are discussed in this book, albeit from another perspective. We have previously alluded to the question of bargaining (and will do so again), some of the conditions under which violence may be employed and, in this chapter, variations on one organization, or political market structure. In the following two chapters, we will treat the matter of organization more fully and the matter of propaganda as well. Skill, to Lasswell, refers to the manipulation of goods, symbols, practices, and recruitment by an elite with respect to the political processes listed above.[18] From Lasswell's formulation, it follows that the permuta-

[17] Harold Lasswell, *Politics: Who Gets What, When, How* (New York: Meridian Books, 1958), p. 112.
[18] *Ibid.*, pp. 31–94.

tions of skills and processes provide one focus for research and theory-building in political science. In this chapter, there has been an effort to conceptualize one of these permutations in a systematic fashion—a permutation involving recruitment and organization. In the case of the less complex formulation, recruitment and organizational pressures produced a system of exchanges that was stable in isolation. The more complex market, however, was less stable and required the involvement of an outside agent, the government, to "solve" the social problem generated by political demands and a recalcitrant elite.

Of course, there is nothing in the nature of things—given other shapes to other reservation demand schedules, the nature or existence of electoral markets, and so forth—that will guarantee a solution to the recruitment problem that will preserve the main outlines of the market. History is replete with cases of elites so jealous of their power and so inept in the skills of political management that they brought about the total collapse of the very institutions and processes that sustained them. Conceive of a case, for example, in which an existing bureaucratic elite is not prepared to meet the social demand for elite positions and in which the government does not, for whatever reason, intervene to coerce a solution.

A relevant case in point concerns the bureaucratic recruitment patterns in prerevolutionary France. There are no simple explanations for the French Revolution, of course; the precipitating events were manifold, complex, and not always obvious. Yet, if one restricts his attention to the administrative recruitment markets of the pre- and postrevolutionary periods, it becomes rather clear that the conflict surrounding exchanges in the civil, church, and military bureaucracies constituted a major engine of social change. Between 1715 and 1787, there had been struck a reasonably stable balance between the supply of aspirants to administrative power (frequently the sons of the bourgeoisie) and the availability of elite positions in the social bureaucracies. Even so, it was a balance that became increasingly tenuous as the revolutionary period approached.[19]

During the eighteenth century, the bureaucracy created by Richelieu, Mazarin, and Louis XIV still managed public affairs from Versailles, and the sovereign, as a consequence, more or less monopolized final control over both foreign and domestic policy. It was a bureaucratic system that was open to penetration from below, with wealth and skill opening the doors to

[19] Extended discussions of the following explication may be found in Alfred Cobban, *The Social Interpretation of the French Revolution* (Cambridge: Cambridge University Press, 1964); Norman Hampson, *A Social History of the French Revolution* (Toronto: University of Toronto Press, 1963); Jeffrey Kaplow (ed.), *New Perspectives on the French Revolution: Readings in Historical Sociology* (New York: John Wiley & Sons, 1965); and Georges Lefebvre, *The Coming of the French Revolution* (New York: Vintage Books, 1947).

important administrative positions. It was a period, then, in which social mobility was considerably greater than is sometimes realized. In addition to the many commoners who held very high public positions, it is estimated, for example, that fully one-half of the French nobility had achieved that status during the preceding two centuries, a tendency that had in fact accelerated during the early eighteenth century. The king could and did raise commoners to noble rank. The policy of selling public offices, especially judgeships, but also financial, military, administrative, and municipal offices, had begun as a revenue-raising device. Social status and public power were exchanged by the sovereign for financial resources, and status was often institutionalized and made hereditary after a certain point. Such was the case, for example, with respect to the Paris law courts, the Parliament, Courts of Accounts, Court of Aids, Great Council, Court of Coinage, and some provincial courts. The same was true of officials in the bureaus of finance, general tax collectors, secretaries to the king (of whom there were hundreds), mayors, and magistrates of certain cities and towns. In short, a rising and ambitious class had assumed, *before the Revolution,* considerable political and administrative power and, while access to such power was based to a great extent upon wealth, it was also based upon skill in the craft of governance. Although the routes of access became increasingly closed after the midcentury period, this point is illustrated by the role played by the bourgeois Swiss banker, Necker, in 1789. Although by then the only nonnoble minister in the government, he alone seemed to possess the skills necessary to keep the monarchy from bankruptcy.

Demands for elite administrative positions during the eighteenth century varied to some extent with economic conditions. Generally, however, demands were increasing, a consequence of the general improvement of business conditions during the period. Improving economic conditions meant that more commoners possessed the political resources necessary to make demands for state employment. (Command over an average regiment, for example, could cost as much as 40,000 livres, a sum that many nobles could not raise.) But the question remained whether or not a sufficient supply of offices would be made available to them.

In contemplating the administrative structure of the monarchy, it is important to recall that both the government and the court nobility were housed at Versailles. Louis XIV had attempted to keep these social groups apart, but it was a separation that was difficult to maintain in practice. Colbert, for example, was of obscure origins, but his son was both a marquis and a minister and his grandson was a duke. During the reigns of Louis XV and Louis XVI, the system of divided social functions collapsed. The court began to move into administrative positions, first gradually and then at an accelerated rate. By 1789, the court nobility controlled all but one ministerial post. By the same year, all the country's bishops, a group that performed many important political functions, were from the same ranks. In short, the reservation demand for elite recruits from outside the nobility had been reached at some point in the century and, as the evidence indicates, *was even shifting to the left.* Roles formerly staffed with members from the Third Estate were now being filled by members of the traditional aristocracy.

Indeed, by the time of Louis XVI, a series of measures were taken to strengthen the social structure against further middle-class penetration. For example, the Sequr ordinance of 1781 restricted army commissions to those who could prove four generations of nobility, and the parlements were tending to recruit their members only from the aristocracy. Certainly it could no longer be said, by the time of Louis XVI, that the monarch was surrounded, in Saint-Simon's terms, only by the "vile Bourgeoisie." The king's household was staffed entirely by nobles, and the minister of war, de Saint-Germain, had ruled that the price of any army position be reduced by one-fourth in order to open up positions for the nobility. More importantly, the *intendants,* those officials in charge of the thirty-four *généralities* (administrative and judicial districts) in France, were now all nobles, holding posts heretofore reserved for commoners or recent nobility. With the heavy bidders for royal office displaced, exchange theory would predict precisely what happened. Offices were "devaluated," setting off a round of competition and bidding among the aristocracy for positions for which, given middle-class wealth, they could not have competed in the past.

In terms of social efficiency, the results were disastrous. Aristocratic office-holders, when not obviously incompetent, were given to political and family intrigues that left them poorly disposed to discharge the public business. A British diplomat, writing in 1788, expressed surprise that such an inefficient government could accomplish anything at all. In any event, these developments produced what our model would have suggested. Social stress and class antagonisms were the result. Under some circumstances, as we have shown, an outside agent might have intervened in these processes to coerce a new social equilibrium in the recruitment market. In the absence of organized and competitive politics, that agent could only have been the king. Constrained as he was by ideology and a deteriorating power base, no such involvement occurred. The lack of effective royal control meant that the bureaucracy tended to embed itself in an ideology of privilege and inertia. Thus, in a period of rapid social and economic change, administration was either conducted routinely or was, more frequently, increasingly moribund. When the king failed to intervene, there was no immediate alternative source of change. And the bureaucracy, designed in part to check the aristocracy, itself became aristocratic. Social tensions continued to mount in the absence of effective forces of conflict resolution. There was no chance, although there were efforts, to resolve the problem in a manner that would have preserved the central dimensions of the bureaucratic system.

Unsuccessful efforts were made, for example, by the provincial gentry. This group had gained little by the Versailles aristocracy's victory (Pyrrhic, as it turned out) in purging the middle class from administration, although it had been promised much. In response, they denounced "ministerial despotism," and cast themselves as defenders of the traditional "constitution." But it proved impossible to shift the reservation demand schedule for recruits of the now entrenched Versailles nobility sufficiently to accommodate even the country gentry. Most employment was reserved for those nobles at the court—some 4,000 to 20,000 out of a total population of some 400,000 nobles. High positions in the church and all ambassadorships were reserved for the court. In 1777, the five military schools founded for the benefit of the provincial nobility were taken over by the forces at Versailles and, in 1788, it was ruled that regimental commands in the army would be reserved for the same forces. In such ways were the aspirations of the Third Estate and the lesser nobility restrained and the stage set for severe social crises. Antagonisms were rising. The *ancien régime,* with its extensive court system and far-flung bureaucracy, had offered employment, wealth, power, and the chance for noble status. The attitude of the administrative and legal middle class changed, under these altered conditions, from hopes of advancement within the system to implacable hostility against it. Two of these men were Danton and Robespierre. The frustration of this class assumed a political character and their bitter opposition to the system led to the fight for reform in 1789.

In a last-ditch struggle to retain the existing administrative recruitment system, the nobles sought remedy in further exclusiveness, in fact, in the institutionalization of their reservation demand schedules. In 1789, at the time of the elections to the Estates-General, they demanded that the creation of nobles through the sale of office be abolished entirely and that the king grant them certain monopolies of employment. On these and other questions no compromise was possible and the Revolution was the consequence.

During the tumultuous years that followed the outbreak of the Revolution—from 1789 to 1830—both temporary and permanent changes occurred in the political, economic, and social exchange markets of France. Enduring changes were forced in the administrative recruitment markets. The extreme centralization of the *ancien régime* was altered and local control of public affairs was emphasized. Local rule involved, during this period, a very large proportion of the population in administration—it has been estimated that some 500,000 people, or 12.5 percent of the total citizenry, held some public office. The judicial system was reformed and rationalized and the popular election of judges and public prosecutors was instituted. In terms of recruitment, the results seem to have been dramatic, although the data is sketchy in many places. At Nerac, for example, all the members of the nobility were displaced as judges and, in all, some 450 million livres were paid out as compensation to the displaced members of the judiciary, suggesting that recruitment patterns were similarly altered in most other areas. In the church, the Civil Constitution of the Clergy abolished the monopoly on high positions that the aristocracy had maintained. Alteration in the elite recruitment markets of the armed forces is particularly indicative. In 1790, the Assembly ruled that one-fourth of the sublieutenants were to be selected from the ranks and the rest chosen by competitive examination. It was similarly determined to open the commissioned ranks in the navy to all classes of society and, during time of war, seamen were to have the right to elect their own commanding officers. Although there was no official purge of existing officers drawn from the nobility, other conditions did force the expulsion or resignation of many. Social divisions in the country were reflected in the armed forces and led to the breakdown of military discipline. The frequent riots of the men in the ranks against their officers led the Assembly, probably more for political and ideological reasons, to side with the ranks against the officer class. The result was the demoralization of the noble officers, which made itself felt in mass resignations. For those noble officers who remained, there was the final humiliation of a loyalty oath which omitted any reference to the monarch. The results were dramatic. By 1792, some 3,500 noble officers resigned from the army, or more than half of all such officers. The same general proportion left the navy, and the social character of the armed forces was thus transformed. The Assembly, the rank-and-file of the armed forces, an ambitious lower clergy, and an aggressive middle-class intelligentsia had intervened in the administrative recruitment markets of the society. The reservation demand schedules of the existing administrative elites were forcibly altered—moved to the right —and the markets themselves were radically restructured.

FOUR

Exchange Conditions in Political Market Structures

We are now ready to examine the characteristics of various political market structures and the manner in which they condition the sorts of political exchanges that occur within them. The structure of political markets is a very important point, since political outcomes will be partly, indeed largely, determined by them. That this is true is attested by the seriousness with which some people take things like constitutions, statutes, treaties, agency regulations, and other less formal "rules of the game." There is a widespread fear of abandoning them for some form of personalized government by one man or by a cadre of men.[1]

The structures of political markets also affect aspects of political performance, as performance relates to the goals of (1) distributive justice or

[1] For efforts to isolate decision-making rules as they relate to specific political processes, see Nelson W. Polsby, "Decision-Making at the National Conventions," *Western Political Quarterly, XIII* (September 1960), pp. 609–619; and Otto A. Davis, M. A. H. Dempster, and Aaron Wildavsky, "A Theory of the Budgetary Process," *American Political Science Review*, LX (September 1966), pp. 529–547.

political equity,[2] (2) the rational calculation or ordering of political priorities, (3) the efficient allocation of resources to their attainment, and (4) the control of power. These subjects will not be treated in any great detail here, but two things need to be said again. First, nothing in the logic of exchange theory suggests that any given political exchange will be a "just" one. In fact, many are not, regardless of how we may intelligently define justice. A reflection on certain economic exchanges makes the point. We may pay more for something, say telephone service, than we think is just. But, because there is only one telephone company, we either must accept the unjust rate, refuse to purchase the service, or, perhaps, work to get the rates reduced by some form of political action. Usually, we "voluntarily" accept the given rate, which is to say that we enter into an exchange with the telephone company and have, at the same time, bowed to the power of the monopolist. It is in this fashion that power and exchange interpenetrate, and it is to the structure of an exchange market, in politics as well as economics, that one should look if he is interested in the question of power. Power, then, consists in the ability to define alternatives; as such it can be given a rigorous operational meaning derived from political market structure.

Second, nothing in the logic of exchange theory suggests that all aspects of political performance are mutually consistent. For example, complete efficiency may be gained only at the expense of centralizing power so far that those in control may curtail the freedom of others. An example of this conflict in goals is apparent in an argument between supporters of a strong centralized federal effort to obtain efficiency and those who prefer a perhaps less efficient local effort which would protect the "freedom" of the locality to make its own decisions. A resulting compromise may sacrifice some efficiency for more local freedom. We do not intend to suggest that all federal efforts are relatively more efficient or that they necessarily impair individual freedom. The point that we wish to make is that the goals of political performance are not necessarily perceived to be consistent.

Thus far in the essay we have demonstrated that exchange can be beneficial to both, or all, trading partners to an exchange. In the last chapter we discussed, for illustrative purposes, a substantive market in which exchange takes place. We did not, however, specify completely the various concepts of market structure, something which we now intend to do. Market structures, as we say, affect the terms of trade, or gains from exchange, between or among those involved in exchange. We can use the economists' notion of market structures as a reasonable analogue to those in which po-

---

[2] See the brilliant empirical study of this question by Walter G. Runciman, *Relative Deprivation and Social Justice* (Berkeley: University of California Press, 1966).

litical activity is conducted. We will not, however, develop any tool of economic analysis that is not useful to our purposes in this book. Therefore, no exhaustive delineation of the economists' graphic depiction of the market place nor the structures of the various classes of markets with which he deals will be presented.

Three classes of markets, as developed by economists, are useful here —the notions of pure competition, pure monopoly, and oligopoly (especially the duopoly situation).[3] Four basic characteristics of social market structures are presented here: (1) the number of actors within the market; (2) the ease or difficulty, or more simply the "conditions" of entry into, or exit from, the market; (3) the nature of the values, costs or rewards, exchanged, in terms of whether they are standard or unique; and (4) the degree of knowledge possessed by those actors within the market.

Pure Competition

Purely competitive political markets, like other socially competitive situations, are characterized, first, by the existence of a large number of political actors within the market. If we are dealing with a market involving some public policy, pure competition presumes that there are a large number of politically involved people who demand the particular policy outcome. They demand that certain outcome because it is among those things that will lead them to their most preferred position. They also demand the outcome because their resources permit them to do so. That is, they are willing *and* able to exchange whatever unit of cost is involved in obtaining the policy or political reward in question, if the other political rewards are not policies. Unless both willingness and ability are present, demand will not be effective—it will simply be latent. For any given outcome, then, all political actors who demand the reward (and, in the competitive case, they are so numerous that no single actor can establish the terms of exchange) do so because they have *effective* demand. They have considered this particular outcome *and* all others, given the availability of other potential benefits and their costs.

Pure competition is also characterized by a large number of actors who are willing to exchange, or supply, the reward present in the competitive political market that they have acquired after undergoing some cost of "producing," or securing, the reward that other actors demand. We have shown earlier, for example, how politicians come to control policies through the acceptance of certain costs. When a sufficiently large number of such

[3] Various economic market structures, including those employed here, are dealt with in Paul A. Samuelson, *Economics* (7th ed.; New York: McGraw-Hill, 1967), Chapter 25, and Richard A. Leftwich, *Price System and Resource Allocation* (New York: Holt, Rinehart & Winston, 1966), Chapters 9–11.

producers of political rewards exist, no single one of them can establish his own exchange ratios, or "terms of trade." Rather, such ratios are determined in the competitive political arena.

Figure 4-1 is used to illustrate this simple point. The equilibrium rate of exchange of the policy, or other benefit, to those demanding it, as well as the costs they are willing to undergo in order to get it, is indicated by equilibrium point E. It is at this point that policy-seekers are willing to undergo cost C_1 to obtain Q_1 of the reward in question. Those who are willing to supply Q_1 of the reward also are willing to accept C_1. The quantity of, say, policy units demanded is, of course, Q_1, and this is precisely the level of policy units that is made available. No actor demanding the policy can obtain it at a cost less than C_1, because all those who exchange the reward can get at least C_1 from the many other actors who also demand the policy. No politician can exchange at any point other than C_1, because other politicians would be willing to exchange at C_1.

Figure 4-1.

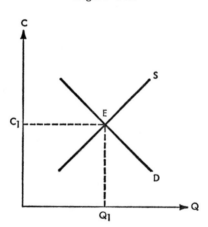

There are other conditions that must be met if a market is to be regarded as purely competitive. A second requisite is that no demander or supplier (e.g., no policy-seeker or policy-maker) may force another out of the political market in question, nor may he create, either formally or informally, a barrier to the entry or exit of other actors into the market. A third characteristic of a purely competitive market is that rewards and costs are standard. That is, the reward supplied by each actor (to those actors who demand the reward) is identical to those supplied to all others. There is no differentiation of rewards. None is unique. This would apply, in economic terms, to a market in which, for example, toothpaste is toothpaste.

No single supplier of toothpaste, if it were exchanged in a completely competitive market, would be able to convince some demanders that his product contained some unique and magical ingredient that would instantly produce success in social ventures. In politics, tax and/or budgetary policies available from many politicians at state, federal, or local levels might tend, in rare circumstances, to meet this condition. The final condition is that each actor must have perfect knowledge of the market. This means that each demander of the policy or other reward in question must have knowledge of the existence of all alternative policies or rewards that may be *substituted* for any single reward. They must also know, with respect to such alternatives, the exchange ratios involved in obtaining all alternative outcomes. The policy-seekers must be aware of the existence of all alternative policy-makers who deal in the single reward in question. In economic terms, the demander seeking to acquire a phonograph set, if phonograph sets are exchanged in a competitive market, must be aware of the existence of all alternative products—television sets, radios, etc., and other products that he might purchase as a "substitute" for a phonograph. Furthermore, he must be aware of the existence of their costs. The demander must, in addition, be cognizant of the various suppliers of phonograph sets, so that he does not secure his benefit at a cost higher than he might otherwise obtain from a competitor of a given supplier. In politics, we could conceive of a tariff policy, or a labor policy, as a substitute for certain tax policies.

When all of these conditions are met, pure competition exists. It is a naïve economist, indeed, who suspects that these conditions prevail widely in the American economy—they simply do not. Nor do they prevail in the polity. However, the purely competitive model is maintained in the economist's toolkit to serve an important purpose. *It is used as a standard with which to evaluate the performance of any given market. This is also its use in political science.* When the actual conditions in a market deviate from the competitive norm, there is a reasonable basis for suggesting that there is a social, political, or economic policy problem, depending upon the sort of market one is concerned to analyze. The competitive norm has long served, however ineffectively, as a basis for antitrust policy in terms of legislation, litigation, and agency regulation. It has been an important political variable. The norm has been accepted because, when the purely competitive conditions exist, certain benefits presumably accrue to society in general. It is one operational definition of the "public interest." These benefits are at least twofold and result in (1) efficiency, by coordinating demand priorities and in allocating resources, and (2) control of the power to coerce, through the maintenance of a decentralized decision-making system. It is not impossible to imagine that these are the same standards that, at least as far as many people are concerned, are often applied to the polity. And it is, furthermore, not impossible to argue (in fact, we insist) that the conditions of political market structures are important determinants of just how much of these benefits accrue to the polity in general (i.e., are widely distributed) and not to specific individuals or groups who may be part of the polity but are in no sense its total membership. In order to *evaluate* the performance of the polity, then, we presume that it is essential to know something about the structure of markets in which political exchange takes place. Market structure is thus an essential societal characteristic that affects exchange—*it governs the process through which people may achieve a more preferred social position.* But which people? That is the question. A better position for a large and powerful policy-seeker at the expense of a less preferred position for a small and weak one? For a powerful politician at the expense of a less powerful one? This matter is one of market structure, and we now turn to an examination of a monopolistic market structure in order to suggest analytics to cope with these questions. We do not, of course, suggest that the classification of markets will, in itself, provide a complete answer to the problem of the allocation of costs and benefits in the polity. What we do insist is that it is utterly crucial to focus on market structures if the problem is to be approached at all.

PURE MONOPOLY

At this point in the discussion of political monopoly we shall introduce some quite simple techniques of analysis and reserve for a later time a more formal exposition.

Many theories of American politics center upon a view of things in which majorities seldom win, most minorities lose, and only a few "veto" groups win consistently. This is one formulation of the doctrine of minorities rule.[4] Although rarely specified very clearly in theoretical terms, a veto group, presumably, consists of a small group (or perhaps a powerful individual) so positioned in the structure of power that it/he can determine whether or not to allocate rewards to those who demand them. Veto groups are regarded very often as subverting American democracy, as contrary to the purpose and intent of the democratic "rules of the game," and as destructive of the "public interest." The basis of such power is varied— sometimes it is held to reside in a few wealthy industrialists or financiers, a trade association, a corrupt and perhaps senile committee chairman in Congress, a political "machine," the "China lobby." With few exceptions,

---

[4] For two contending formulations of this matter, see Robert Dahl, *Preface to Democratic Theory* (Chicago: University of Chicago Press, 1956) and John C. Livingston and Robert G. Thompson, *Consent of the Governed* (New York: The Macmillan Co., 1963), Chapter 6.

and regardless of specific sources of power cited, the veto group is seen as thwarting the processes of democracy.

We have no quarrel with certain of these formulations, including their evaluative dimensions. It is less frequently recognized, however, that such groups have precisely the same theoretical significance as do the more obvious, but less frequently criticized, constitutional veto groups that exist.[5] All such groups have one thing in common: In the pure case they effectively control a particular area of public policy. For that reason, they can determine, within limits, who in society, if anyone, will benefit from their power. A congressman's control of sugar import quotas, a state governor's clemency power, or the President's power to intervene unilaterally in the affairs of other societies are all cases in point. The reader will think of other examples.

Of course, the pure case is rarely found; the more typical case involves a sharing of power of some sort. In any case, however, where one or a few men working in concert control the allocation of policies, any theory of competitive politics will require modification. We are brought, then, to consider the political situation characterized by monopoly.

In the monopoly case, all actors are not free to pursue policies available at many points in the structure of decision; rather, their options are two. They may exchange with the sole allocator of policy or not at all. But there are mitigating factors, stemming largely from the fact that the *extent* to which political monopolists may be said to have power depends upon the extent to which policies of nearly the same character can or cannot be secured elsewhere in the polity. Citizen groups have often played off the Corps of Engineers against the Bureau of Reclamation, both of which are in some sense monopolists in terms of the type of dams they build in the western states.[6] The dams may be substitutable. To the extent that they are, there is a decrease in the power of each agency. In fact, there are often many substitute rewards in politics. Rivers can be developed also by state resource agencies, local cooperatives, or private industry. In each case the policy in action would be somewhat different, of course, but the point is that where there are many substitute rewards, the power of the monopolist diminishes and the situation approaches the competitive one. In such cases, it is somewhat easier for actors to secure policies more efficiently. While recognizing the rare occurrence of pure monopoly in most

[5] Charles Beard argues in his famous *An Economic Interpretation of the Constitution of the United States* (New York: The Macmillan Co., 1913) that the formal decision-making rules of American politics were designed to provide for minority, or elite, rule.

[6] Arthur A. Maass, "The Kings River Project," in Harold Stein (ed.), *Public Administration and Policy Development* (New York: Harcourt, Brace, 1952), pp. 533–572.

political systems, we consider the pure case below in order to show its implications for the more normal case in which substitutes exist in varying degrees.

The pure political monopoly situation is one in which those individuals who control the allocation of specific policies for which there are no substitutes are the only ones who do so and is one in which no one else is permitted, for whatever reason, to enter the market as a purveyor of the same policies. For example, the ubiquitous conflict between the appropriations subcommittees and the substantive committees in the Congress is often a struggle over who will have power to allocate particular policies, each committee in each set determining to remain, or become, a political monopolist.[7]

Unlike competition, then, monopoly assumes that there is one large and powerful actor in the market and that he has the power to establish, within certain limits, the ratio in exchange between costs and rewards. Normally this actor is assumed to be a supplier (such as the sole supplier of an economic good or a one-party system in which all policies of importance are decided by the ruling party). We shall operate for a moment with this assumption and discuss the problem in terms of monopolistic policy-makers (politicians) dealing with nonmonopolistic policy-seekers. We further assume that the monopolist inherits his power from past performance. We do not, however, dwell on this point but rather focus on his exercise of power.

The political monopolist, we assume, has further power. Not only is he the only policy-maker in the system but he also has the power, we have said, to prevent the entry of potential competitors. In economic terms, the monopolist may do so either by acquiring (by contract or by integrating with suppliers) exclusive control over the resources required to create the reward in question. The political monopolist may also prevent entry by controlling the distribution of the policy involved (in the same way that the economic monopolist can), thereby preventing other policy-makers from offering the policy at a competitive exchange ratio. Constitutions, laws, and other agreements are often the empirical expression of the power to prevent entry. In addition, as the sole allocator of a particular policy, the political monopolist is, in effect, dealing with a unique policy. There may be, as we pointed out earlier, substitutions for the policy, but each substitute is in some way different from the one provided by the monopolist. For example, if the monopolist is supplying policy X, no other reward is precisely similar, although at some point policy Y would be, for some

---

[7] Richard F. Fenno, Jr., *The Power of the Purse: Appropriations Politics in Congress* (Boston: Little, Brown, 1966), pp. 34–35, 43ff., 72–73, 113–122, 149, 469–472. For some genuinely new propositions concerning House-Senate exchange patterns, see Chapter 12.

policy-seekers, a substitute for X. The point would be reached where the exchange ratio of costs for policy X became so high that they would begin to substitute Y for X. Nevertheless, the monopolistic politician is still in an advantageous position. He does not have to worry about other politicians supplying X. And we must remember that, under some circumstances, *no* substitutes of a meaningful sort exist: there is no substitute for peace when the alternative is total war. Normally, however, the monopolist must take into account the reaction that policy-seekers would exhibit if he chose to supply on terms that would put the policy-seekers in a less preferred position than if they accepted the somewhat inferior substitute, policy Y, but at a "better" exchanged ratio than that pertaining for policy X.

The monopolistic politician may, or may not, be able to affect the information possessed by the policy-seekers with respect to the policy he controls. He may choose to use some of the resources, which his power permits him to acquire, in order to convince the policy-seekers that policy Y is indeed an inferior policy, or inferior substitute, for policy X. He may do so, normally, not by informing policy-seekers of the actual conditions that pertain to policy Y, but rather by putting policy Y (or, more typically, its suppliers) in a false position. This is not an unusual aim of political propaganda, although it is not the normal expression of advertising in the economy. In the economy, most advertising focuses the viewer's or reader's attention on the alleged superior qualities of rewards such as X. Such gentleness is less frequently exhibited in political debate, even though the venting of political spleens seems to be declining.[8] This is a deplorable development for those people who are fond of the excitement, drama, and vitriol of political debate. It seems to be the case that Democrats, like economic advertisers, are fond of "pointing with pride" at their alleged achievements, while Republicans are more given to "viewing with alarm" the same activities. Logically, they cannot both be right, although both may most certainly be wrong.

Figure 4-2 is useful in depicting the performance of a monopolistically structured market and in contrasting the monopoly and competitive outcomes of alternative structures.

Given the number of policy-seekers in the market, their preferences for various policies, and the availability of policies as well as their costs, demand schedule D shows the alternative policy units demanded at all costs of policy X. Schedule S shows the various units of costs of supplying policy X at each level supplied. Cost C_1 and policy level Q_1 would be an equilibrium attained through competition if many weak politicians were in the market and each was forced to accept the decisions of the policy

[8] William C. Mitchell, *The American Polity* (New York: The Free Press of Glencoe, 1962), p. 378.

Figure 4-2.

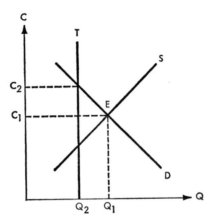

market made in a decentralized manner. But with one politician dominating the market, it becomes possible for him to set his own cost/policy output position for policy X. In the previous chapter, we used the concept of a reservation demand curve (T) for a particular reward–the quantity of bureaucratic elite appointments. Now we are prepared to deal with a representative policy, X, for which we do not offer a precise description. It could range from a public expenditure to a political symbol. But what we do wish to show is that under competitive conditions there would be a market solution different from that reached under noncompetitive, in this case monopoly, decision situations. If we were still employing the notion of a reservation demand curve, we would note that the political monopolist would offer less than Q_1; he would offer Q_2. And, in addition, he would demand that those wishing the policy pay a higher cost, in this case C_2, which is greater than under competitive conditions C_1. Later, in Chapter V, we will more formally derive the most sought-after solution that the political monopolist wishes to achieve. However, prior to doing so, several points must be noted.

First, if a policy-seeker, such as fiduciary A, must pay the higher cost C_2 rather than the competitive cost C_1 for some policy X, he is in a less chosen, or preferred position; this can be demonstrated with the use of our indifference analysis. Examine Figure 4-3. Note that with a given quantity of resources to be used to obtain two policies, X and Y, the line of attainable combinations shifts from C_1 to C_2, indicating that the individual must pay a higher price, or meet a higher cost, to get X. This shifts him from indifference curve I_1 to the lower curve I_2, and from point C to D. The lower curve represents a less preferred position and shows that a higher price must be paid for one reward.

Figure 4-3.

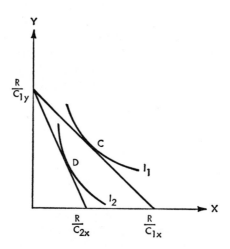

Referring back to our box diagram (Figure 1-8) in Chapter I, we are able to see that the distribution of rewards has shifted in favor of B at the expense of A. Individual A, in this case the policy-seeker, or a typical one, has moved back toward *H*. Individual B, the monopolist, has moved to a more favorable position toward *H,* or away from his relatively less preferred position at *G*. (Again, note that individuals A and B might be beneficiaries, fiduciaries, or politicians, depending upon the market analysis.) In this case, the political monopolist is rewarded *not* because he is an efficient organizer of the political market, but rather because he possesses and exploits monopoly *power*. He operates from a power position and he may or may not enforce his power position over time through its use, a matter that depends less on the analytic devices used to explain political markets than on the myriad of conditions that pertain in each market. But insofar as the monopolistic politician is rewarded for power, or, what is the same thing, the ability to enforce a centralized decision-making process, he has thwarted the system's ability to generate both political equality and freedom. Equality is thwarted because he has exercized power and has pushed the policy-seeker farther from the perfectly equitable point, distribution point *G*, and back toward *H*, and has himself attained *H*; freedom because he has created a centralized decision-making market, a creation he will presumably maintain or seek to maintain.

We wish to emphasize an earlier observation: economic and political markets are often characterized by neither perfect competition nor by pure monopoly. They more often lie somewhere between these polarized positions; they are oligopolies. Oligopoly is a situation in which there is more than one but less than a fully competitive number of actors on the supply side of a market. We could note that the basic economic markets in this country are of this character—steel, aluminum, automobiles, etc. However, we could not hope in this volume to articulate the many types of oligopolistic structures that exist in the economy, either those depicted in the market models of the economists or those which have been empirically described and analyzed. A similarly large number of political oligopolies exist that could be described empirically or modeled conceptually. The latter is a task of great magnitude, and we are hopeful that some readers of this book will help in its resolution. We turn now to a discussion of one most useful oligopolistic market model, one which fits uniquely the analysis of a two-party political system—the model of duopoly.

Prior to dealing with this point, it should be noted that what we have done thus far is to show the benefits of competition and the policy problems that arise when political monopolies exist. In Chapter V, we offer a more formal and rigorous description of decision-making in a political monopolistic structure, which we urge the reader to examine. The formulations just offered, and those that follow, we believe to be helpful, but we caution against accepting the analytics that we outline in this essay as acceptable alternatives to the detailed study of existential markets. The behavioral propositions that will most realistically describe political behavior must be discovered empirically.

POLITICAL OLIGOPOLY AND DUOPOLY

We turn now to the least determinant aspect of the polity and the exchanges that occur within it and within the system of economic reasoning we are employing here. The problem is an inherently difficult one, and our discussion of it is intended less to solve it fully than to outline its dimensions. We refer to the oligopoly market structure, a structure that is intermediate to the extremes of competition and monopoly. An oligopoly exists when outputs (goods in the economy, policies in the polity) are controlled by a few producers (firms or politicians). Thus, the market structure of oligopoly may be distinguished from that of perfect competition and monopoly in the following way: First, perfect competition is composed of many individuals and is independent of the control of any one person; second, in the monopoly case, one person controls the entire market, that is, the market "price" and output; and third, in an oligopoly, a few entities control the entire market and, most importantly, the actions of any one entity will affect the other entities because the "price" set by any one entity will affect the demand for the output of all others.

We found that in a perfectly competitive market all entities supply a given reward and that the reward of one politician is indistinguishable from those of all other politicians. Each perfectly competitive entity produces a standardized reward, that is, each reward is a perfect substitute for any other. Under monopoly conditions, however, one entity alone satisfies a given market. In a monopoly there is no exact substitute product available—the monopolist's output is unique to the market. In an oligopoly, a small number of entities control the market, and each of the several produces an output that is a close substitute for those of the other entities. The four basic characteristics of an oligopoly are as follows: (1) several entities share control of the market—each entity sets its own exchange ratio according to its own view of the market, and each entity determines its own output; (2) each entity offers an output that is somehow distinguishable from the outputs of other entities; (3) it is difficult for new entities to enter the market because of the existence of restricted access; and, (4) there is usually imperfect knowledge of the market.

In economics, the major distinguishing characteristic of oligopoly is the fact that a limited number of firms control the market. Thus, the term *oligopoly* could apply to a large number of actual market situations. The only limitation is that there cannot be so many firms in the market that the actions of any one firm will go unnoticed by the other firms. As long as the price and production decisions of any given firm have a direct effect on the demand faced by the other firms, oligopoly will exist. One firm in an oligopoly may act as price leader, setting prices that the other companies will follow. Other methods of preventing severe price competition are also followed. Beyond this, it is important for oligopolies to restrict entry into their markets. Methods employed by oligopolies to prevent entry into markets are similar to those employed by monopolies. One method is to control resources, and the other is to establish "patents." If one firm develops a patent on a product, process, or production technique, it is protected from competition in that particular area. The reader will see the theoretical similarity between patents and political rules—in fact, patent laws *are* political rules. Also, an exceptionally large "investment" may be required before a new entrant can compete in an existing market. In politics, this is similar, among many others, to the third-party problem.[9] The large investment is not only due to the cost of the plant and facilities necessary to produce, but also to the cost of advertising needed to develop new markets. The problem of advertising in politics will be taken up shortly.

Finally, like monopoly, oligopoly is not characterized by a complete absence of market knowledge. The oligopolist must tell the buyer enough about his product to interest him, but he will give the consumer only information that is favorable to his particular output.

[9] E. E. Schattschneider's treatment of this issue is still unsurpassed (*Party Government* [New York: Holt, Rinehart & Winston, 1959], pp. 69–98).

Oligopoly market structures are situations often found in politics. Its characteristics are most obvious in the case of situations involving two serious competitors, or what is called duopoly.[10] The duopoly case has a wide range of applicability in politics. Although there are other oligopoly situations in politics, we will not emphasize them, since the duopoly case represents all the problems of all cases in their essential aspects. The most obvious duopoly case, and the one used here for illustrative purposes, bears on the functioning of the two-party system in the American polity. The analysis of two-party politics that we undertake here gives faint reason for accepting the notions of some political scientists and political sociologists that competitive two-party politics comprises the essence of democratic politics.[11] Such ideas rest on the view that each party, in the struggle for office, will give the public what it wants and that the "outs" will keep the "ins" responsive to the desires of the community.[12] This is what is meant, in sociological terms, by the competition of elites for mass support. There is nothing in the logic of duopoly situations that compels these sorts of relationships; other "solutions" are quite as possible, a fact that, in our judgment, requires skepticism toward much of the literature that defends so strongly two-party systems. We shall explain why this is so.

Oligopolistic markets are characterized by what economists call "circular interdependence." In the system to be discussed, we shall assume two major sets of policy-makers. The loosely disciplined parties in the

[10] William J. Baumol, *Economic Theory and Operations Analysis* (Englewood Cliffs, N.J.: Prentice-Hall, 1965), pp. 327–337.

[11] Joseph Schumpeter, *Capitalism, Socialism and Democracy* (New York: Harper & Brothers, 1947), Chapter 5; Seymour M. Lipset, *Political Man* (Garden City, N.Y.: Doubleday, 1960), pp. 45–46; J. Roland Pennock, "Responsiveness, Responsibility, and Majority Rule," *American Political Science Review,* XLVI (September 1952), pp. 790–807; Ernest S. Griffith, *Congress: Its Contemporary Role* (New York: New York University Press, 1951), pp. 156–157. A debate is involved here: Schumpeter and Lipset emphasize the responsive (within limits) character of "competitive" party systems to what we would describe as the political resource markets; Pennock and Griffith are fearful of "too much" responsiveness, or the "irresponsibility," of competitive party systems. As we show below, *either* outcome—elite rule or majority rule—is a possible outcome of duopoly politics. *The structure itself imposes no determinant outcomes.* For this reason, much of the debate about party systems misses the mark. For other treatments of the issues we discuss here (none is consistent with our analysis) see Austin Ranney and Willmoore Kendall, *Democracy and the American Party System* (New York: Harcourt, Brace, 1956); Austin Ranney, *The Doctrine of Responsible Party Government* (Urbana: University of Illinois Press, 1954); Pendleton Herring, *The Politics of Democracy* (New York: Farrar & Rinehart, 1940); *Toward a More Responsible Two-Party System,* Report of the Committee on Political Parties of the American Political Science Association (New York: Rinehart, 1950).

[12] Anthony Downs, *An Economic Theory of Democracy* (New York: Harper & Brothers, 1957).

American system fit this requirement. Let us assume, then, that both the majority and the minority party in the market make policy. This is certainly true in the United States and, in fact, it is sometimes difficult to determine which party is major and which is minor, for example, when one party controls the Presidency and the other the Congress; or when the governorship and the state legislature are split between the two parties in some way; or when each party controls one house of a bicameral parliament. But even when one party is clearly major, that is, when it staffs all organizing roles in the formal organs of government, the minority party must often be consulted as, for example, in those cases where constitutional rules require some majority vote greater than 50 percent plus one (for example, treaty ratifications) for a decision and when the majority lacks that number of votes. In other words, policy-making is typically shared in the American two-party system. Other ways in which the "minor" party counts will occur to the reader.

Let us then conceive of two parties involved in making decisions with respect to the same policies. Let it further be assumed that, in the case at hand, the politicians of each party are concerned to secure votes; indeed, they want all the votes that they can get, given some restraints on cost. But we know from the prior logic of this book that in order to get votes the politician must allocate policies, the control of which involves an expense to politicians. Now what may the parties do in such a situation? The answer to this question explains precisely why it is that the oligopoly problem offers few determinant solutions. They may do a number of things. In the case of political competition the axioms of exchange analysis describe rather exhaustively what will occur under stated conditions. To say, then, that political parties in a two-party system may do a number of things is to say that they cannot take the conditions under which they operate for granted. This is so because the conditions, or parameters, of the political market shift, or may shift, with each decision made by either party. This is what is meant by circular interdependence. If Party A does x, Party B may or may not do y, or perhaps may or may not do z. In no case will Party A be very sure of Party B's response. Party B, of course, is equally unclear about A's intentions. All of this simply means that members of duopolies cannot be very certain about even the immediate future— decisions are always made in a misty environment. From the perspective of exchange theory, of course, this means that it is impossible to specify the "best" decision for either party. In short, each party wants to secure enough votes to win (in either the short or long run) and to expend only as many resources as are required to be the winner, but each must remain uncertain as to how that purpose is to be achieved. (The reader will observe that this uncertainty contains the ingredients of political change, simply because the decisions made in the indeterminant duopolistic political market will affect the structure of decisions in other markets.)

Let us examine the problem in more detail. Examine first the decisions that Party A may make. It may determine its exchange ratio (so many policy units in return for so many votes) without regard for Party B's presence in the market. But such a decision involves certain dangers. After all, Party B may choose to offer a "better" exchange ratio to the electorate, thus taking away all of Party A's votes. Republicans, it seems, often accuse Democrats of "under-selling" them. Party A could, by ignoring B, be eliminated from the market, and Party B would become a political monopolist. We may assume, then, that Party A will not automatically choose this course of action. Another tactic would be for Party A simply to adopt any pattern of exchange set by Party B. This would presumably at least maintain Party A in the market—it is a survival tactic. Or Party A might attempt to establish the ratios of exchange between votes and policies in the hope that Party B would follow suit. If Party B does acquiesce in following the lead, then Party A is in a particularly rewarding position since it can set the exchange ratios at a point that will place it in its most preferred position. Still another tactic is to involve Party B in a struggle for political survival—thus, Party A might attempt to establish exchange ratios that Party B, given its cost structure, cannot offer. If successful, Party A would emerge as a monopolist and thus be free to follow the exploitive prerogatives of the monopolist. But what if Party A should lose the fight to the finish? All would be lost, and Party B would emerge as the monopolist. In addition, and before making the decision to enter a zero-sum fray, Party A would have to consider the costs involved in such a struggle, costs that, combined with the possibility of losing, might inhibit such an all-or-nothing tactic from being followed. Still another possibility, one that introduces still more ambiguity into the market, is for Party A to accept the exchange ratios established by Party B but to try, at the same time, to offer virtually costless rewards to its clientele—perhaps by conducting the exchange with voters more rapidly or by offering the voters more poetic political propaganda. But, regardless of the tactic chosen, Party A can never choose a tactic that it knows will lead it to its most preferred position. All of its decisions must be based upon what it believes Party B will do, and of that it can never be sure. A hypothetical example will make this point somewhat clearer.

Let us consider a case in which parties A and B are similar in all significant respects: size, costs, ideologies, and votes. Put differently, we assume that when both parties establish the same exchange ratios, each gets one-half the values in the market or, in this case, one-half of all votes. Each party thus confronts the same demand structure for public policies.

Each party also, following the logic of exchange theory, has certain costs. Thus, if each party is willing to allocate the same level of policy units in return for the same level of votes, it is possible to establish an exchange ratio that will move both political parties to the most preferred position possible. Let us call this exchange ratio position *PP* (for most preferred position). The exchange rate in question might, then, be taken as the point of equilibrium between the two parties. But this is not necessarily the case, since there is nothing in the logic of the situation to induce the parties to remain at that point. Thus, there may be no equilibrium point at all in the duopoly case. Everything depends on how each party views the other. If each party refused to recognize the other as a market participant, however, then exchange rate *PP* would indeed be set and would remain set as long as the nonrecognition lasted.

Other decisions, however, might be made. Suppose, for example, that Party B is determined to try to improve its position by moving from *PP* to a still more preferred position, that is, by moving to a higher indifference curve. This entails taking some voter support from Party A, which in turn requires that Party B offer policies at a cost lower than *PP*. The success of this maneuver depends upon Party A's not lowering its exchange rate, obviously a very dubious proposition. Party A may very well lower its exchange rate to the same level, and, if it does, then Party B's decision has been self-defeating. Indeed, both Party A and B have moved from a more to a less preferred position. Subsequent decisional outcomes are similarly indeterminant. It might be the case that Party B, seeing the folly of having lowered its exchange rate, would move its rate back to *PP*. If Party A follows Party B's action, then, of course, point *PP* is re-established as the equilibrium point of exchange. But the parties are not, after all, in collusion (we are not discussing monopoly), and therefore there is no reason for Party A to follow Party B back to *PP*. By not moving back to *PP*, Party A will be in the same position that Party B was when Party B first lowered its exchange ratio; that is, Party A is now in a position to obtain some of Party B's support. To prevent further erosion of its own position, Party B might very well shift back to Party A's lower exchange rate. In such circumstances, neither party can easily increase its exchange ratio, realizing that the other party may not follow the lead. The point is now made clear: No optimal exchange rates can be established in duopoly markets. It is rational for each party to maintain the lower exchange ratio arrived at through the process just described, just as it was rational at an earlier point for each to maintain exchange ratios at point *PP*, and as it was rational for one party to attempt to improve its position at the expense of the other. From all of this, a certain paradox emerges: If one party decides to lower the exchange ratio still further, the other party must very likely follow suit. Thus, there is a large number of decisional outcomes, any one of which may establish an equilibrium in the market, with the decisions of one party vis-à-vis the decisions of the other being responsible for the variation. Thus, the way in which decisions "react" to decisions becomes important to an understanding of duopoly political structures. Reaction analysis, so called, has been used in economics to study the duopoly problem. While it does not in fact solve it, reaction analysis does shed important light on the issue. For that reason, it is useful to indicate how reaction analysis might partially explain certain of the recurring problems in understanding political duopolies such as two-party systems, two-set interest groups, and other forms of political oligopoly.

REACTION ANALYSIS AND DUOPOLISTIC POLITICS

To illustrate how reaction analysis bears on political understanding, let us return to the analytical elements just discussed, that is, the case of the two-party political system.[13] Let us now assume that Party A has established some rate of exchange for votes and policies. As we noticed in the above discussion, it is quite likely (although not necessary) that Party B will react to Party A's exchange ratio. Let us assume further that both parties control the same sorts of policies and that demand for these policies by voters is perfectly responsive to shifts in the costs of policies as established by the politicians. Under these rather stringent assumptions, both political parties will want to allocate policies for votes at the same exchange ratio. Thus, if one party lowers the ratio, the other will follow. A number of such shifts as we noted above would establish a series of exchange ratios, any one of which could be an equilibrium point. But we might also relax these assumptions and imagine a slightly more imperfect market, one in which demand for policies is not perfectly responsive to costs, and in which either party will retain some voter support even if it offers its policies at costs greater than those of the other party. The reader will observe that, with these new stipulations, we approach somewhat more closely the actual operation of the American party system.[14] These relaxed and more realistic assumptions enable us to employ reaction analysis. In Figure 4-4, the curve A is Party A's reaction curve; the curve B is Party B's reaction curve. What do the curves express? Curve A indicates that for every exchange ratio (policies for votes) established by Party B, there is an exchange ratio

---

[13] Baumol, op. cit., pp. 327–337.

[14] For discussions of intensity and party support, see Jack Dennis, "Support for the Party System," American Political Science Review, LX (September 1966), pp. 612–613, and Philip E. Converse, Aage R. Clausen, and Warren E. Miller, "Electoral Myth and Reality: the 1964 Election," American Political Science Review, LIX (June 1965), pp. 322–325.

that Party A will want to set. If Party B should establish low policy costs, Party A will want to establish a somewhat higher ratio. Party A will, of course, lose some portion of voters who have heretofore supported it, because the party now fails to meet the competition of politics; that is, it fails to meet Party B's exchange ratio. But, we recall, the market is to some extent imperfect. Therefore, some portion of Party A's support will remain loyal even at Party A's higher exchange rate. In the real world, some portion of voters (e.g., "convinced" Republicans or Democrats) find it very difficult to change their party affiliations, whether from habit, ignorance, social pressure, or whatever. But this is true only at low exchange rates; political changes do occur, after all. At high exchange rates set by Party B, the reverse will occur: Party A will choose to set ratios below those of Party B, given the reasonable assumption that, at high exchange levels, voters are more responsive to differentials in exchange ratios. Even many of the staunch loyalists depart, as they do, for example, in so-called critical elections for the parties, such as 1860 or 1932.[15] Thus, Party A may exchange policy at a lower rate than Party B, but, as they say, it makes it up on the volume.

If we examine the 45° line in Figure 4-4, we will notice that some portion of Party A's reaction curve falls on either side of the line. Party B responds to Party A much as Party A responds to Party B. This is shown by curve B. Curves A and B intersect at point E, and an equilibrium is achieved that represents identical levels of what both political parties will exchange in the way of policies for votes. This is shown in the figure: When Party B establishes a policy cost at BC_2, Party A will set its costs at AC_2. Party B is then encouraged to remain at BC_2, and Party A has no reason to shift from AC_2. Thus, at this unique point, each party reacts to the other in a manner that produces stability in interparty competition; we would seem to have arrived at a solution to duopolistic political conflict and to have explicated the structure of decision-making in this political market. However, the usefulness of this explanation is obscured by the fact that it seems to rest on certain premises concerning how each party views the other, premises that border upon being contradictions. Specifically, reaction analysis anticipates that each party will expect the other to maintain his exchange ratio. This, if Party B sets policy costs at BC_1, then Party A will set policy costs at AC_1 with Party A's decision reacting on Party B, who establishes a new ratio, which reacts on Party A, who alters his ratio, and so on until some equilibrium point is reached. This process suggests that,

---

[15] Classifications of types of elections vary to some degree. See V. O. Key, Jr., "A Theory of Critical Elections," *Journal of Politics*, XVII (February 1955), pp. 3–18; Angus Campbell, Philip E. Converse, Warren Miller, and Donald E. Stokes, *The American Voter* (New York: John Wiley & Sons, 1960), pp. 531–538.

as each set of moves occurs, each party must find out that the other party's ratio is not a stable one. But reaction analysis assumes that each party believes the other party's position to be a stable one. Perhaps all we can really say is that if point E is reached, by whatever process, equilibrium is achieved, but that, once again, the decision-making process of getting to point E is indeterminant. A more adequate analysis would have to take

Figure 4-4.

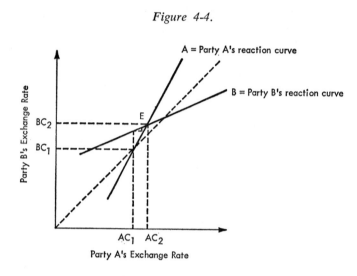

into account how any set of decisions, by either party, affects decisional premises of the parties vis-à-vis each other.

OLIGOPOLY AND THE PRINCIPLE OF POLITICAL EXCLUSION

We now discuss one other important aspect of political oligopoly. In the above discussion, we assumed that each political actor in the duopoly situation was concerned only with the consequence of his decisions upon the decisions of his competitor. We may now complicate the analysis somewhat in an effort to answer the question: What maintains the oligopolistic structure in politics? Why do not new competitors—new political parties or new interest groups—enter the market? In answering this question it becomes clear that, actually, each oligopolist must set his exchange ratios not only in the presence of other actors in the market, but also in such a way as to discourage new competitors from entering. Given the logic of our formulations, what, then, sustains the two-party system, or the two-member fiduciary set, or any other oligopolistic political markets? We recognize the many efforts of new political parties to enter American politics,[16] and while we are less informed about the growth, number, and policy interests of interest groups in American history,[17] we are familiar also with new groups attempting, sometimes successfully, to enter a particular policy market. We are impressed, however, with the stability of many oligopolistic political structures in American politics, and it is this durability that may be analyzed through the concept that we explicate here, the concept of political exclusion.

In discussing the question of the durability of oligopolistic political structures, let us consider a duopolistic fiduciary market. (We could continue with the discussion of political parties if we so chose since the logic is identical in both cases; we discuss fiduciaries simply to show how the analysis of oligopoly can be applied to other political actors.)

One thing the reader may have noticed on the basis of the foregoing discussion of political oligopoly is that, while there was no basis upon which the actors could make optimal decisions, there remained, on reasonable assumptions, only two oligopolists in the (party) system. Of course, the number could have been somewhat larger, and the conclusions we developed would still hold. Thus, while oligopoly is peculiar in the sense that not all conditions in the market are known, there were still some known and stable elements in the system, for example, the number of actors. The stable element that interests us here concerns a fixed number of political oligopolists in a set. We also pointed earlier to a potential series of decisions in the oligopolistic political market leading to the establishment of lower exchange rate (no series leading to higher exchange rates was possible). Yet we know that there is an absolute floor that limits the degree to which exchange rates may go without abolishing the oligopolistic structure; that is to say, no political party can survive in the long run if it establishes exchange ratios at a point where it receives less from voters than the party must return to them in policies. The same principle will apply to fiduciaries in similar political structures.

Thus fiduciaries have a floor of exchange ratios but, in duopolistic

---

[16] In the conventional political science literature, perhaps the two best treatments of party exclusion are to be found in Schattschneider, *op. cit.*, Chapter 5, and in Maurice Duverger, *Political Parties* (New York: John Wiley & Sons, 1955), pp. 216–228. They emphasize, of course, the single-member district with plurality election system as an *explanation* of two-party systems. John G. Grumm, "Theories of Electoral Systems," *Midwest Journal of Political Science,* II (November 1958), pp. 345–376, is closer to the logic of exchange theory in suggesting that such a system is an exclusionary *tactic* and is installed by already dominant elites.

[17] Some relatively recent data is contained in Murray Hausknecht, *The Joiners* (New York: Bedminster, 1962), on membership rates, but there is, apparently, no available census of all political interest groups in the United States.

and other oligopolistic structures, they do not necessarily have a ceiling, if a ceiling is defined as an optimal exchange ratio. This principle we have already discussed. This less-than-entry exchange ratio would obviously confront any new fiduciary who might consider entering the political market in question. Now it is reasonable to expect that oligopolistic fiduciaries will not welcome new fiduciaries into "their" markets. We assume, however, that they have no constitutional means, as politicians do, of restricting the entry of new competitors.[18] Still, it is apparent that no new fiduciary can enter—because he will not survive—if the long-term policy costs in the political market exceed long-term beneficiary contributions.

Consider one case in which a new fiduciary is considering entering a particular policy market. There is no necessary reason for any potentially new fiduciary to assume that he will be a more efficient operator than the existing least efficient fiduciary who, himself, may be operating in the market on break-even terms. No new fiduciary will enter the political market if he must establish a cost for the policies that he will secure for his beneficiaries that is to some degree more than beneficiary contributions.

But it is also possible that a new fiduciary, who can conduct his affairs just as efficiently as any existing oligopolist, may consider entering a particular market. Under these conditions entry might indeed be made, even though there are arguments that it will not, at least under some conditions. The argument is one that goes to the question of scale. Suppose that the fiduciaries in question are national in the scope of their operations and their beneficiary membership. Thus, there may be a minimal, and quite large, scale of operations required for participation in any such political market. If the potential new fiduciary's scale of operations is too small, his "unit" cost will be too high for efficient competition. In an oligopolistic market, it may also be the case that any one of the few quite large interest groups in the political market controls a significant portion of the policies in the market. The result is obvious: There is no room in the market for new fiduciaries, even though there are no formal mechanisms of political exclusion, and even though the exchange ratios in the market are very attractive. Entry would mean, for both old and new fiduciaries, that to secure policies at the least cost, more and more policy units would have to be secured, but they would have to be offered to beneficiaries at lower and lower costs. Thus, the exchange ratio in the policy market would fall and, given the economies of scale, some fiduciaries would be eliminated. Of

---

[18] In addition to such devices as the establishment of single-member districts, plurality systems, other electoral rules serve to limit competition. Examples would include poll taxes, filing fees, preregistration, residency requirements, provisions governing access to the media, and the requirement that a party receive a certain share of the vote in the preceding election (e.g., 10% in Colorado) before it can automatically appear on the ballot.

course, it might not be the new fiduciary, but it is quite possible that it would be. Under this set of probabilistic outcomes, then, the task that faces existing oligopolistic fiduciaries is to set an exchange rate that is just sufficient to discourage a potential fiduciary from entering, building a new, large organization, and wreaking havoc with political stability. What they may do, then, is to secure policy units for distribution to beneficiaries at a level so that the additional policies secured by an additional fiduciary would bring beneficiary contributions below the cost of policy units due to the new beneficiaries. All of this is important to an understanding of the exchange ratios—the policy-securing and the contribution-demanding decisions—of oligopolistic fiduciaries. If we establish at what level of policies oligopolistic fiduciaries will undergo costs to secure in their effort to prevent entry by new fiduciaries, we will also be able to know what they will demand from their beneficiaries in return for policies.

At this point, it is necessary to digress for a moment with this observation: Not all political competition occurs between parties. An obvious example was the campaign within the Democratic Party for its 1968 presidential nominee. In essence, Senator McCarthy's bold New Hampshire bid was a challenge by a political entrepreneur, here a competing politician, to an established politician. Senator McCarthy overcame many implicit barriers to entry and entered this "marketplace" offering, however tenuously, a new political reward (his vastly different approach to foreign policy). With the breaking of these entry barriers, the market was expanded to include more competing politicians, more resources, and a much broader marketplace ranging throughout the country.

Senator McCarthy's challenge had the effect of making a change in United States policy toward Vietnam a "legitimate" reward to seek. This also had the effect of bringing angered and frustrated spectators into the political process as both beneficiaries and fiduciaries. *The New York Times* quoted from a description of this event on May 13, 1968, "Suddenly there's hope among our young people . . . Suddenly they've come back to the main stream of American life." When significant barriers to political participation are created and maintained, some people will feel powerless and disenfranchised. Their resulting disillusionment and frustration may lead to violent actions to destroy the system's structure, and this in turn may lead to equally violent reactions to maintain the system—especially its power structure. These barriers may be imposed either by the system's rules (such as voting age restrictions) or illegitimately, as exemplified by the legion of acts restricting the American blacks.

In this chapter, we have outlined three major decision-making structures within which political goods are exchanged and allocated: pure competition, pure monopoly, and duopoly, the latter being a major and representative case of oligopoly. We have shown how these political market structures bear on the issues of efficiency, freedom, and the manner in which power and structure interpenetrate. We have also shown that skepticism must be maintained with respect to the conventional propositions relating to two-party systems and these same values. In addition, we have addressed ourselves to the matter of market stability, or political exclusion, in an effort to explain the durability of formal and informal political institutions and processes. In these tasks we have utilized simple supply, demand, reaction, and indifference analysis.

In Chapter V, some parts of these same problems will be examined from another angle of vision, specifically the economic theory of the firm. We shall introduce additional analytics that are at most points consistent with our past methodology, but which, in these circumstances, appear to offer keener insight into the process of political decision-making and the allocation of political costs and benefits. Again, we will introduce only those economic concepts that seem relevant to our problem of political analysis and will not be concerned with the full logic of the methodology as developed in economics.

Before proceeding with this task, however, we must enter a qualification. As we have said, we do not intend in Chapter V to equate political theory entirely with the analysis of the firm's behavior. We do believe, however, that to employ the theory of the firm in the analysis of the behavior of political entrepreneurs (a term to be used in the next chapter) is useful in two respects: (1) It enables the analyst to focus on the political entrepreneur's dual decisions regarding which rewards to seek and which resource-expending tactics to use; and (2) it permits the observer to focus on the exchange of rewards and costs in political marketplaces. An alternative analytical device is provided by game theory, which permits analysis in terms of expected net payoffs; that is, the expected rewards in various markets less the resource costs expended to achieve the expected rewards. Game theory deals with a matrix from which the political entrepreneur might choose in an effort to maximize his rewards or to minimize his costs. However, it does not go "behind" the matrix to deal with the points raised in (1) and (2) above.[19]

[19] Baumol, *op. cit.*, pp. 529–549.

FIVE

Exchange and Political Entrepreneurs

We have dealt thus far with certain problems facing every polity: (1) What output priorities are to be satisfied? (2) How are input resources to be mobilized to satisfy the demand for these policies? (3) For whom are the output priorities met? In previous chapters we have discussed these questions in a number of ways and we have concluded that their answers depend upon (1) the distribution of wants (tastes and preferences) among the members of the polity, (2) the level and distribution of political resources among members of the polity, and (3) the manner in which political markets are structured. The key roles associated with these matters, as we have identified them, are played by beneficiaries, fiduciaries, politicians and, often in a more passive sense, the audience. All of these role-players are crucial to the operation of the polity. But one role—the fiduciaries'—is susceptible to treatment from an analytical perspective that allows one to analyze systematically the process whereby resources are mobilized to satisfy demand priorities. We can focus on the fiduciary, understood as a catalytic political agent, through the use of the economist's "theory of the firm." In this chapter we may, then, examine the decisional problem that confronts the political fiduciary, the role-player who is in some sense the basic demand articulator and resource organizer in the polity. This is *not* to say that he is necessarily the most powerful actor in the polity; that question is determined by market structure. It is to say only that he provides the link between most political resources and most public policies.[1] This point must be emphasized.

THE FIDUCIARY AS ENTREPRENEUR

The Resource (Input) Markets

The fiduciary requires resources in order to secure policies of interest to his beneficiary membership. How he is to secure such resources, then, becomes a major problem to be faced. Consider a fiduciary's demand for a particular resource, say a larger membership, something that is often sought by political interest groups and that is universally regarded as a political resource.[2] As before, we conceive of his demand for new members as a *potential* fiduciary decision. But we are also aware that for each new member that the fiduciary induces to join the association he must give something to them. This means that he must divide any policy he secures from the politicians or other fiduciaries into smaller "shares" for distribution to an enlarged membership. The fiduciary is faced with a familiar problem: Can he get more from a new member than he has to give up to him in policy units secured from politicians or other fiduciaries? Consider the two variables involved in this case: (1) the value of new members induced to join the interest group, and (2) the additional policy units that the fiduciary must allocate. We may invoke the following principle in answer to this problem. The fiduciary will balance the value of a new member against the units of policy that must be allocated to each new member. But what is the value of a new member? This answer is really given in conventional interest group theory, even though it is rarely expressed as such. *It is the value of the additional power that each new beneficiary contributes to success in securing policies from politicians or other*

---

[1] This is the manner in which, in our view, the political functions of interest groups may be understood most rigorously. The best-known studies of interest groups include Arthur Bentley, *The Process of Government* (Chicago: University of Chicago Press, 1908); David B. Truman, *The Governmental Process* (New York: Alfred A. Knopf, 1955); Harmon Zeigler, *Interest Groups in American Society* (Englewood Cliffs, N.J.: Prentice-Hall, 1964); and Earl Latham, *The Group Basis of Politics* (Ithaca, N.Y.: Cornell University Press, 1952).

[2] Mancur Olson, Jr., *The Logic of Collective Action* (Cambridge, Mass.: Harvard University Press, 1965), *passim*. According to Olson, such a notion may well be in error; we agree (and comment further in footnote 10), although our view is less strict than Olson's.

fiduciaries. Or at least this is the case from the viewpoint of the prudent fiduciary. If the power contributed by the new beneficiary to fiduciary success in getting things from politicians is greater in importance than the policy units that must be allocated to the new beneficiary, then the fiduciary will attempt to attract a new member. This is the basis for the fiduciary's demand for beneficiary members. By following this decision-making logic, the fiduciary could determine how many, if any, new beneficiaries he should attempt to recruit—he relates his demand for these "recruits" to his cost. In this manner, the demand for political resources, in this case membership, can be determined. The same sort of analysis would provide the demand for other resources that fiduciaries require in their struggle for public policies, for example, size of beneficiary dues, prestige of members, skills of staff members, size of public relations budgets, and so forth. While this is the sort of logic involved in the pure case, it is more likely that, actually, fiduciaries answer these problems not in terms of one additional member or one additional staff expert but rather by making judgments about a *range of resources* and the *range of demands* that will follow the attraction of additional political resources (as well as a *range of policy* that can be demanded by new resources in what we will call the policy markets).

The Resource and Policy (Output) Markets

Viewed from the perspective of the fiduciary, and given his support resources, the political "goods" market imposes two requirements. He must first operate on a day-to-day basis with political reality, dealing with the exigencies, the shifts and tides of politics, as he finds them, and at the same time attempt to maximize his position—and by definition his beneficiaries' —within the constraints and disciplines of that reality. However, the fiduciary is not, cannot be, indifferent to his long-run fate; as a consequence, his day-to-day decisions may reflect a greater concern with the long-term problems of group autonomy, group growth, and group safety than would appear reasonable from a short-term perspective. That is, his short-term behavior may be such as to *appear* imprudent and conducted at the expense of obtaining policies apparently more directly and immediately tied to the interest of the group. This is one reason why ostensibly liberal, or even radical, political groups often behave rather conservatively. Our contention is that it is compatible to view these sorts of short-term decisions as consistent with fiduciary and beneficiary interests. The second major problem of concern relates to the manner in which one is to understand the behavior of the fiduciary in politics at any point in time.

His short-term problem is to settle upon some level of policy units to demand (and to decide how to use his resources in order to get them). In the short run, where certain of his resources and costs are fixed, these decisions are made with the realization that he (the fiduciary) *cannot increase his political apparatus, his resource base, without some time-lag.* The long run, by definition, is that period during which such alterations can be made.

The short-run problem, then, is a tactical problem. This is the allocation issue, or how one is to use resources already at hand in the pursuit of policies. In politics, there are frequently (although by no means always) many options available to the fiduciary. He may concentrate the bulk of his resources in a few political markets, say the judicial market (as did the NAACP in the first desegregation cases);[3] the electoral market (as does the League of Women Voters);[4] the parliamentary market (as do many economic associations);[5] or he may spread his resources widely in a large number of such markets (as did the AMA in combating President Truman's health care proposals in 1948).[6] In the short run, policy costs are fixed and known, producing the tactical problem of choosing that tactic that will secure policies at the least cost.

To settle upon a tactic, the fiduciary must consider how to *combine* his resources in such a fashion as to obtain the policies in question at the least cost. He may bribe politicians, erect billboards, or donate funds to a political campaign, but regardless of his tactics, he will choose that combination of resources that is most efficient. Thus, it is the cost involved in any combination, or ordering, of resources the fiduciary possesses that will determine, in part, the political market(s) that he will enter in his search for policies, and what tactics he will follow in those markets. In American politics, the federal system, with its separation of powers, or sharing of powers, at national, state, and often local levels, is organized in a manner often consistent with this analysis. That is, the *same* policies are often available from the *different* policy-makers who staff the disparate policy markets

---

[3] See Clement E. Vose, "Litigation as a Form of Interest Group Activity," in S. Sidney Ulmer (ed.), *Introductory Readings in Political Behavior* (Chicago: Rand-McNally, 1961), pp. 209–221.

[4] Although the League enters other markets, such as parliamentary politics, Lewis A. Dexter, "What Do Congressmen Hear: The Mail," *Public Opinion Quarterly*, XX (Spring 1956), p. 7, it may do so without much success; Frank Bonilla, "When is Petition 'Pressure,'" *Public Opinion Quarterly*, XX (Spring 1956), p. 46.

[5] R. Joseph Monsen, Jr., and Mark W. Cannon, *The Makers of Public Policy* (New York: McGraw-Hill, 1965), discuss the tactics of a number of economic interest groups. Also see Raymond A. Bauer, Ithiel de Sola Pool, and Lewis A. Dexter, *American Business and Public Policy* (New York: Atherton, 1963). For a study of interest groups in the constitutional rule-making markets, see Lewis A. Froman, Jr., "Some Effects of Interest Group Strength in State Politics." *American Political Science Review*, LX (December 1966), pp. 952–962.

[6] David Hyde and Payson Wolff, "The AMA: Power, Purpose and Politics in Organized Medicine," *Yale Law Journal*, LXIII (May 1954), pp. 1010–1018.

in the political order.[7] That this is not always the case, however, was emphasized in the discussion of political monopoly in Chapter IV.

Through calculations such as these, the fiduciary arrives at an answer to his tactical problem. His actual problem, however, is considerably more complex, and is made more complex (if we remember that his resources are not undifferentiated) by the fact that he must choose a combination of resources that will move him to a more preferred position and not just any combination. In other words, some resources are more productive and cost more than others and, therefore, must be rewarded with policy units of commensurate magnitude. Economists would refer to these different resources as factors which vary in their productive capacity and costs.[8]

We may get at the nature of this problem by posing the following question: What would likely happen with respect to a heretofore "good" tactic if the availability of one resource became less costly and with no change in the resource's productivity? What would happen if a resource, say membership dues, could be increased without any decline in membership, or membership support, and without any need to secure more policy units for the increased dues received from members?

Here we assume that the cost of one resource has declined but that the cost of other resources remains unaffected in quantity and quality. The wise fiduciary would be encouraged to substitute the cheaper resource (an increase in membership dues without any obligation to pass on greater policy units to beneficiaries) for some other resource. The consequence of so doing may be to shift from the former policy market(s) to a new one(s) in which to secure appropriate policies. For example, a partial shift might occur from the parliamentary to the electoral market, resulting in a new effort to "lobby" the electorate rather than, as formerly, the politicians; for example, he has more money to spend on billboards, a more preferred tactic. But such a solution is rarely completely substitutable for access to politicians in the parliamentary market. Resources may only be substituted to a certain extent since lobbying before parliamentary bodies cannot be ignored completely. In other words, as the fiduciary begins to substitute one resource for another, his new tactic will presumably pay off; it will not, however, pay off indefinitely. At the point where rational substitution becomes impossible, the fiduciary will have located his new market tactics. This suggests another political fact: Even if a resource becomes available

[7] See William Riker, *Democracy in the United States* (New York: The Macmillan Co., 1965), pp. 310–314.

[8] Paul A. Samuelson, *Economics* (7th ed.; New York: McGraw-Hill, 1967), Chapter 23; Richard H. Leftwich, *The Price System and Resource Allocation* (New York: Holt, Rinehart & Winston, 1966), pp. 98–116; and William J. Baumol, *Economic Theory and Operations Analysis* (Englewood Cliffs, N.J.: Prentice-Hall, 1965), pp. 250–258.

at lower cost to fiduciaries, fiduciaries will likely be constrained against complete substitution of one resource for another.

Having dealt, however briefly, with the tactical problem that faces the fiduciary, we may now attempt to answer another and related question. After he has selected a market to enter in pursuit of policies, what *level* of policies will he seek there? We recall a familiar proposition: The fiduciary engages in politics in an effort to maximize his personal position, and this maximization will consist of some level of resources contributed to him by beneficiaries minus those resources allocated by the fiduciary in securing policies from the government. To do this he will choose a tactic in the manner shown above. But he must also answer the other half of the question, which relates to the level of policy units he should expend resources in securing. In other words, what balance of costs and benefits will maximize his position within the market? We trust that it is not too confusing to say that this question raises further questions. Specifically, they relate to the costs of policy units as well as to the maintenance, or increase, of beneficiary contributions, and the relationship between policy units and the costs of securing those units. When the fiduciary has resolved these problems, the level of policy units he will seek is known: He will seek that number of policy units where there is the greatest difference between total beneficiary contributions and total policy costs. Such a decision would maximize the fiduciary's position, since the difference between contributions and policy costs is that portion of social resources he retains for himself. The analytics used here will vary somewhat from those we have used previously.

Let us first discuss the relationship between policy units and the cost of such units. Let us once again also invoke short- and long-term considerations. Short-term fiduciary costs are those costs that can be varied in the present, according to the number and costs of resources used in securing policy units being pursued by the fiduciary. Thus, by altering the policy units sought, the fiduciary will alter his short-term costs. But he cannot vary all of his costs even though he, for instance, reduces his demand for policy units; to do so might eliminate him permanently from the political system. For example, the fiduciary may not be able to reduce salaries of experienced and politically well-connected staff members and still survive to fight another day. This is the case because of what are known to economists as fixed costs. They are incurred regardless of the level of political activity by the fiduciary. Staff members have talents saleable in the market place, and they will not accept an arbitrary reduction in personal resources. For these sorts of reasons, our short-term analysis may be restricted to a concern with the relationship between policy units and variable costs, or costs that can be altered in the short run by the fiduciary.

It will be recalled from the discussion of the tactical problem that the

fiduciary is free to combine resources in any manner and that, for each level of policy or reward units obtained, it was possible to locate the most efficient combination of available resources. Now, if we know these points, it is possible to obtain the average cost for each policy unit, or the average variable cost plus the average fixed cost. These averages are attained simply by dividing policy or reward costs by total policy or reward units. For example, average total cost = total costs/policy units; average variable costs = variable costs/policy units; and average fixed costs = fixed costs/policy units.

Why is this interesting? Because it permits us to establish the relationships between any level of policy units the fiduciary might seek for his group with the expenditures of resources transferred by beneficiaries on those policy units. If we were to graph this as is done in economics, average total, average fixed, and average variable cost schedules would be relevant.

Average total cost is the sum of the average fixed and average variable costs. Initially, average policy costs decrease per policy unit until a certain point is reached, at which time a negative effect sets in and average cost per policy unit begins to increase. Why should this be true? As policy units are first sought, it is possible to combine variable resources with increasing efficiency because of the progressively more specialized and differentiated role structure within the organization. Sophisticated policy-getting requires sophisticated policy-getters. Progressively more policy units can be obtained with each incremental employment of a variable resource. Average variable costs are thus decreased per policy unit. Average fixed costs also decrease. As the fiduciary secures more and more policy units, the fixed costs, such as the salaries of crucial staff members, are spread over more and more policy units. Also, staff skills and energies may be more fully utilized until, at some point, their talents are being fully exploited. But the reduction in average total cost does not continue indefinitely. It will become progressively more difficult to organize and coordinate the activities of more and more variable resources. This will, we assume, at some point require progressively more resources to "produce" incremental units of a reward or policy. This will eventually increase average variable cost and will do so at an increasing rate. At some point this increase in average variable cost will more than offset the continuing decrease in average fixed cost. Average fixed cost will obviously decrease at a decreasing rate. For example, if a key staff member's salary of $100.00 is allocated to one policy unit, the average is $100.00; for two units it is $50.00; for three units it is $33.33; for four units it is $25.00; and for five units it is $20.00. As the units increase, their average fixed cost decreases, but, as is apparent, at a decreasing rate.

One might have thought, impressionistically, that the fiduciary would

secure that level of policy units where the average total cost is at a minimum. But this is not necessarily the case. We must consider the extremely important marginal principle discussed earlier. Here marginal cost pertains to the *additional* variable cost of securing *one* more policy unit. Marginal cost is secured from the relationship between total variable cost and marginal cost: Specifically, when diminishing returns set in and as average variable cost falls, marginal cost rises. And when average variable cost rises, marginal cost rises at a more rapid rate. Marginal cost is equal to average variable cost and to average total cost at that point where these costs are minimized.[9]

We may now answer the question: What level of policy demands will maximize fiduciary welfare? Where marginal revenue (beneficiary contributions) and marginal costs of policy units are the same, a fiduciary will demand the level of policy units available at that point. At that point, his gain will be maximized or his loss minimized. The validity of this observation is demonstrated by conceiving of a level of policy units greater than this common point. At any such level, marginal cost would be greater than marginal revenue; to demand policy units at such levels would result in diminution of the resources that a "successful" fiduciary is free to retain for himself. Alternatively, conceive of a level of policy units demanded less than at this common point. At any such policy level, marginal revenue will exceed marginal costs. Thus, the fiduciary can increase beneficiary contributions by moving to a point where marginal costs and marginal revenues are the same.

THE FIDUCIARY
AS A MONOPOLISTIC ENTREPRENEUR

We have now determined the relationships between the resources that a fiduciary must expend in exchange for a certain level of policy units. But to answer the question as to what level of policy demands will maximize fiduciary welfare we must first ask: What is the relationship between the beneficiary resource contributions to the fiduciary and his resource cost? That is, what does he have left over? What a fiduciary hopes to secure are resources from beneficiaries that are at least equal to his costs. The fiduciary will receive beneficiary contributions at a level either less than, equal to, or more than the costs of the policy units he secures. Which of these contributions he in fact receives will depend upon his political market *power*.

Figure 5-1 depicts the fiduciary as a monopolist—the only supplier of a policy which is in some sense unique. The demand curve represents the

9 Samuelson, *op. cit.*, Chapter 24; Leftwich, *op. cit.*, pp. 126–151; and Baumol, *op. cit.*, pp. 263–266.

Figure 5-1.

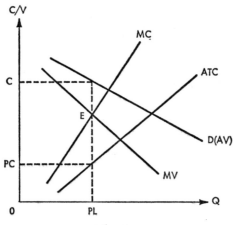

Policy Units

D:	quantity of policy units demanded by beneficiaries
ATC:	average total cost of supplying the policy units incurred by the fiduciary monopolist
MC:	marginal cost of supplying the policy units
AV:	average value of policy units demanded by beneficiaries
MV:	marginal value of policy units demanded by beneficiaries

alternative quantities of the policy that beneficiaries want at various policy costs. The demand curve represents also the average cost at each alternative quantity of the policy. Recall that in the discussion of demand curves in Chapter III we pointed out that they are downward sloping. Thus, people will demand greater quantities of the policy in question only at lower costs, or they are willing to pay progressively lower average costs. This means that the policy-suppliers, the fiduciaries, receive progressively lower average value (AV)—the resource cost to the beneficiary is the resource value received by the fiduciary. We can now calculate the important marginal value (MV) curve for the fiduciary. It is the change in the total value of resources exchanged to him by beneficiaries for one unit increments in the policy that he exchanges to them. Since the beneficiaries are willing to exchange only at progressively decreasing average resource costs (or values), the total resources exchanged, or total value (TV) received by the fiduciary, is increasing, but at a decreasing rate. In fact, the rate of decrease of the margin is more rapid than that of the average. For example, consider the following numerical series shown in Table 5-1.

We know that to maximize his own welfare, the fiduciary will offer a

TABLE 5-1

Resource Cost or Value per Policy Unit

Quantity of the Policy Unit	TV	AV	MV
1	10	10	—
2	18	9	8
3	24	8	6
4	28	7	4
5	30	6	2

quantity of policy units that will equate his marginal value (obtained from resources received from contributing beneficiaries) with his marginal resource cost incurred in obtaining the policy units. In this sense, the fiduciary does not "produce" rewards himself. He obtains them elsewhere—a matter we shall discuss directly. We note that since this particular fiduciary is a monopolist, he can establish whatever exchange ratio with beneficiaries he wishes. Since he is a monopolist, he is the only source through which beneficiaries can obtain the *specific* policy reward in question. Other less preferable rewards may be obtained elsewhere, but not this one.

Marginal value received and marginal cost undertaken by the fiduciary are equal at quantity of policy units PL in Figure 5-1; that is, they intersect at point E. Note that at this point, the average total cost incurred in obtaining each unit of quantity PL is PC. However, the average resource cost that the beneficiaries are willing to give up for quantity PL is C. The reward to the fiduciary is $(C - PC) : PL$. In essence, he receives more value expressed in terms of resource units than he gives up to obtain the policy units. This is his reward—but is it competitive? The answer is No. This is based on our definition of the costs in the ATC curve—they include *all* average fixed and average variable *costs* including the normal competitive return to the fiduciary. His return, or reward, then, is more than that which would have come about under competitive circumstances. But he has, we assume, the power to attain and maintain a market position that is monopolistic. He has the power to convince beneficiaries that he is unique and unlike other fiduciaries, or that the policy he supplies is unique and unlike other policies. He also has the power to create barriers against the entry of new competitors (who might offer lower exchange ratios, that is, "undersell" him). He is powerful enough, in some way(s), to prevent external pressure (e.g., government or other fiduciaries) from regulating the structure of "his" market or his conduct within it.

The impact of this power has, first, resulted in a less efficient coordination of demand priorities and resource mobilization than would have been the case under competitive political conditions. Second, the fiduciary has been rewarded not for his political ability, *but for his power*. Third, market

power remains centralized, and he has used this power, we assume, to propagandize for the view that he, or his policy, is unique (which it may not be objectively) and thus has reduced the cognizance of beneficiaries insofar as other alternatives are concerned. In keeping potential competitors out of "his" market, he has prevented the emergence of other alternatives. He has, as importantly, forced beneficiaries to give up more resources to get a given quantity of policy units. In terms of indifference analysis, beneficiaries find themselves in a relatively less preferred position than would otherwise be the case. This is so because of the fiduciary's power.

The reader will observe, now, that this analysis of the political monopolist is very similar in kind to the analysis of political monopoly discussed in the last chapter. We have varied the analysis somewhat in this chapter to demonstrate a more formal application of economic theory in political analysis.

THE FIDUCIARY
AS A MONOPSONISTIC ENTREPRENEUR

The fiduciary may extend his power in another direction—into the markets where public policies are "produced" or made available. Recall that we discussed the exchange between beneficiaries and a fiduciary in terms of beneficiaries' units of a policy. Now we may analyze the process by which the fiduciary "receives" the policy units he allocates to the beneficiaries. We presume for the moment that he is large, powerful, and the only securer of this policy. Such instances are obviously rare in the pure case. But consider, for example, a sizable number of local politicians eager to accommodate the only large industrial firm in a community. Such conditions often result in favoritism, expressed perhaps in preferential tax rates, or an unwillingness to apply wage or safety or zoning legislation to the industry in question, or in some other policy form obtained by fiduciaries and passed on to beneficiaries. At the national level, examples are fewer because of the many fiduciaries normally interested in the same policy; for instance, it is less preferentially allocated to one fiduciary. This is so even though politicians often act as if they were competing for a single policy-seeker: Terms such as the "farm bloc," the "South," "labor," "big business," the "Polish vote," and so forth, testify to some tendency to view certain policy decisions as important only to a monolithic interest. Our problem is to explain the matter theoretically in terms of exchange.

Central to the meaning of fiduciary power is the fact that the fiduciary can, to some extent, determine what resources he will exchange to the politician for particular public policies. (He also, to some extent, controls the exchange rates between beneficiary contributions and policy units allocated to beneficiary welfare.)

Suppose, for example, that the fiduciary could lower the average resources he had to spend in order to obtain some quantity of policy units, such as *PL,* given in Figure 5-1. To the extent that he is in a position to do so, there is a downward shift in the average total cost curve. That is, each quantity of the policy, including *PL,* can be obtained by the fiduciary at a lower average total cost. Depending upon the power relationship between the fiduciary and the beneficiaries, the beneficiaries would pay a lower average total policy cost for more policy units. That is, some portion of the "savings" would be passed on to the beneficiaries. But the extent to which the fiduciary is a monopolist will define the extent to which he will pass on rewards. The more powerful he is, the less of the savings he will pass on to beneficiaries, and the more of the reward he will keep for himself.

The politicians, we have seen, in a case in which they exchange with a monopsonistic fiduciary, are placed in a less preferred position because the politician receives fewer resources, on the average, for any quantity of policy he exchanges to the fiduciary. Given the political power of the politicians vis-à-vis competing politicians, they might be able to pass this "cost" on to the audience; for example, they might establish a higher "tax" from which the audience may or may not have an alternative. The alternative is supplied by the existence, or lack of existence, of alternative politicians from whom the audience may be free to choose. But the audience may not object to the higher tax. If the policy that eventually is obtained by the beneficiaries has benefits external to those beneficiaries (benefits commonly shared by the community in general), the audience may be willing to pay the tax. We reach at this point an incredibly complex system of political linkages. This or any other volume simply cannot delineate all of them, which is why we have selected to analyze these few markets. We cannot do more here than to state in summary the following. The primary articulators of demand priorities are fiduciaries and politicians. They also organize and mobilize resources, or inputs, and from this organization, outputs, or policies, are obtained and distributed. Individuals share in the benefits of obtaining outputs and escape the penalties of giving up resources, depending upon their power. Their power depends upon the decision-making resources they can acquire and their "position" in the structure of political markets. The greater an actor's "stock" of resources and his monopolistic or monopsonistic power, the more preferred position he is able to attain (and maintain). Thus, the exchanges between and among beneficiaries, fiduciaries, politicians, and the audience are conducted voluntarily in order that they may attain a more preferred position.

But if a sufficient number of actors attain a slightly more preferred position through exchange, and if others attain dramatically more preferred positions, envy or jealousy may intervene. This alone may produce aliena-

tion sufficient to "endanger" the system's maintenance. This would be especially dangerous for the keepers of the system *if* an alienated minority of the dispossessed also exists and can be mobilized by radical reformists in loose or formal coalition with those who wish somehow to improve their "lot" relative to others but see no hope of so doing. How do those in power prevent these conditions *or* this mobilization? A typical method is to propagandize in order to maintain the system against radical change.

Each market decision-maker (each politician or fiduciary) has some unique control, in the case we are discussing, over certain values (policies or other rewards) at stake in the market in question. This market structure is in part determined by political camouflage and propaganda. It may also be determined by collusion.[10] But in any circumstance, propaganda and ignorance are crucial to its perpetuation.

Perhaps some portion of beneficiaries and the audience *believes* that its welfare can be maximized only through the activities of a *particular* fiduciary or a *certain* politician. None of this may be true objectively, but we are not, after all, dealing with omniscient political actors. The result is obvious: Any particular actor in the market may act *as if* he controls some unique value of importance and, to the extent that such an actor may act in this fashion, a monopolistic or monopsonistic element is in fact introduced into the market. More realistically, some actors are not deceived with respect to the real facts of the matter (they know that similar policies or whatever are available elsewhere), and the market structure will actually reflect some competitive elements.

We may inquire in more detail as to the factors that give rise to such a political structure. Political distortion and propaganda are important reasons, as we have said. Beneficiary A may believe that only fiduciary B is in the business of securing favorable political decisions for, say, veterans, or

---

10 It is appropriate to note here that when we refer to monopoly or monopsony we mean something that may be somewhat different from the usual denotation given those terms in economic analysis. We presume a monopolist *either* is a single individual or the result of a "tightly knit" collusive agreement between or among two or more actors. While the structural arrangements may appear to differ in these two cases, when there is perfect coincidence of interests and complete discipline among those in collusion, the analytic, and we presume actual, results are the same. However, if the number of individuals in a collusive agreement is relatively large, the likelihood of wants being coincidental and the probability of perfect discipline is reduced correspondingly. This may serve to induce certain individuals to "go on their own" and to compete with their former associates, or it may serve merely to make the agreement more "loosely knit," thus permitting a certain measure of personal autonomy. In any event, one thing is clear: If there are few actors it is easier to collude than if there are many. This is why it is important for monopolists and monopsonists to create, whenever they can do so, barriers to exclude potential political competitors. Olson, *The Logic of Collective Action* is relevant to this point, especially Chapter 3.

farmers, or dock workers, while, in fact, fiduciaries C and D are interested in securing the same policies for beneficiaries and the audience in general. This is one reason, an important one, why interest groups make such great efforts to point out their (so they say) unique policy interests. So, too, for the same reasons, fiduciaries may be blind to the fact that, in addition to politician A, politicians B and C are in a position to make policy decisions of importance to fiduciary interests. Politician A and fiduciary B, in such circumstances, clearly enjoy some favorable control over political outcomes. Their monopolistic power is limited, however, to the extent that others in the market are not deceived. (In fact, society has assumed certain costs in an effort to make clear which political markets are open and which are closed, by underwriting the education of a class of people, lawyers, whose business it is to know the extent to which politicians, and which ones, control any given market.) We may express this general proposition differently: It is the case in such markets that a politician or a fiduciary will continue to receive some contributions even though the policies or other values he controls are available at lower exchange rates from other actors in the market. Under perfect competition, as we know, contributions to any actor are perfectly responsive to market, which is to say political, pressure. In a less perfect market, however, contributions are not perfectly responsive. Since either actually or perceptually (the result is the same) the politician or the fiduciary deals in slightly different policies or other rewards, they are not, precisely speaking, political competitors. We may, by modifying slightly the economist's vocabulary, refer to the set of political actors dealing in slightly different policies as the monopolistically competitive political group.

PROPAGANDA IN THE POLICY

Let us now consider the decisional problem that faces the monopolist, that is, the propagandist. Let us assume that one member, say a politician, can be taken to represent all the problems of all members of this type of monopolist. (Again, we could just as easily focus attention on the fiduciary, because the logic is the same in both cases.) Consider the politician's problem: He must pick a level of policy units that he will allocate to fiduciaries and, at the same time, settle upon the level of contributions he will demand in exchange for such units. He will select those levels that will maximize his own returns. But we have already alluded to one additional matter that complicates the analysis, or at least the politician's analysis. The problem is referred to in economics as "selling" or advertising costs; in politics, as we have pointed out, the expression "propaganda" costs might well be used. While we mentioned the matter earlier, we discuss it in more detail now in an effort to explain one reason for the massive propaganda that exists in politics.[11]

Any politician in the monopolistic political structure must convince potentially interested fiduciaries that he (the politician) does in fact monopolize some share of the policies present in any given policy market. He must do so by engaging in propaganda or other efforts to deceive at least some of the people nearly all of the time. Political exchange theory assumes that this will involve a cost to the politician. This additional cost, also and obviously, will affect the demand for the policies he may allocate. The reader will note that this introduces a new decisional problem: To what lengths must the politician go to convince others of the unique position he either does occupy in the policy-allocating process, or of the position he wishes to appear as occupying? The cynic might answer that he would go to any lengths, a judgment derived from the apparent experience of some people. But since we are committed to an analysis of exchange, we must take issue, however reluctantly, with such a conclusion. We must assume that he will undergo *some* propaganda costs, since only by doing so may he retain some monopolistic control in the political order. We may, therefore, separate the normal costs the politician assumes in getting and retaining political office from the costs he will assume in getting some level of monopoly control associated—even potentially—with that office. Of course, the politician's total costs will simply consist of both his propaganda and his normal costs. If the reader prefers to think in existential terms, he might think of an "inside dopester," or a political "boss," political types who attempt to persuade others that only through them can people get what they want politically. When people learn otherwise, the power of such politicians collapses. Muckrakers and other social reformers have often directed their energies toward making people aware of alternatives in politics and the deceits practiced by ostensibly monopolistic politicians. This is what is meant by educating the people.

Propaganda costs influence the market in a number of ways, ways that have consequences for the politician's decision-making. (1) Such costs will cause the demand schedule for policy to shift; that is, more policy units will be demanded at each level of cost. (2) They will also, in the normal case, alter the configuration of demand; that is, those demanding the policy will assume that there are fewer genuine substitutes for the policy. (3) They will, as we say, increase the politician's costs. Awareness of these factors enables us to analyze more fully the decisional problem confronting the political propagandist. We may do this by remembering that propaganda

11 For a brief but insightful statement on the relationship of propaganda to policy, see Alfred de Grazia, *Political Behavior* (Glencoe, Ill.: The Free Press, 1952), pp. 359–360.

costs are undertaken by the politician in order to enable him to receive more contributions in exchange for policy than would be possible in the absence of propaganda. However, to engage in propaganda means that the politician's cost in controlling policies increases. The politician will continue to engage in propaganda as long as the additional resources expended in such efforts are *at least* equal to the additional contributions made to him.

Figure 5-2.

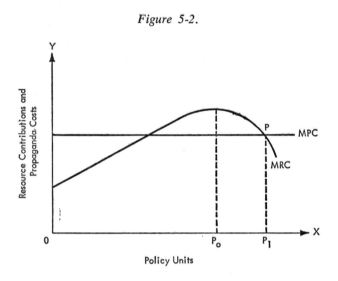

Policy Units

Figure 5-2 conceptualizes the problem graphically. The Y axis represents units of resource contributions to the politician and units of propaganda cost. The X axis represents the additional number of policy units. The marginal propaganda cost curve (MPC) represents the *addition to cost* that the politician is prepared to undertake for each addition to any policy level given at the zero intercept. For the sake of conceptual simplicity, we assume that for each addition to any given policy level, the marginal propaganda cost is the same (or a horizontal line). In fact, other behavioral propositions would result in other slopes to other MPC curves.

The marginal resource contribution curve (MRC) represents the addition to the politician's resource base caused by changes in any given policy level from that represented by the zero intercept. From 0 to P_o, we presume that some people are increasingly responsive to propaganda. They are willing to exchange increasing amounts of resources to the political propagandist for constant increments of policy. But, at P_o, something important happens. Only empirical research can say what this is. But, speculatively, one may reasonably assume that people become progressively less willing to exchange resources for the policy. That is, for each constant increase in the policy they are prepared to exchange progressively fewer resources, hence the downward slope in the MRC curve. But why? Saturation with the policy is a likely primary explanation. Other not unreasonable explanations would derive from disillusionment, possibly flowing from a new awareness of the misrepresentations of political propaganda. This is the credibility gap. Still another possibility is that policy-seekers have been captured by countervailing misrepresentations—more clever myth-makers or, in some systems, purveyors of "the big lie."

We are now presented with a familiar answer to the question: What changes in the level of policy units is the politician willing to allocate that enough people are willing to accept? The politician will establish the levels where marginal propaganda costs equal marginal resource contributions and where people will accept this level. Point P in Figure 5-2 shows that the optimum level for the politician is quantity P_1—it is also the market equilibrium.

We may examine the meaning of these facts for both fiduciaries and politicians who enjoy such favorable exchanges as a consequence of their privileged positions in the political order. In the case of fiduciaries, we would expect new and aspiring fiduciaries to enter politics. In fact, new fiduciaries will enter, given the logic of exchange theory, until marginal costs equal marginal contributions for all fiduciaries in any particular market. Such a development would result in the erosion of monopoly power on the part of any particular fiduciary. This is a partial explanation for the origins of interest groups, although we have previously shown that entry may be prevented by a variety of exclusionary techniques.

In the case of politicians, of course, entry into the market is even less likely, given constitutional and other legal constraints on the expansion of policy-making positions in the polity. There is only one U.S. President, nine members of the Supreme Court, a fixed number of Congressmen and bureau chiefs, and so on. One may not simply choose, regardless of his political resources, to become the 536th Congressman (although with sufficient resources he might very well displace an existing one). Still, authoritative formal positions in the polity do expand: The original Congress had only 90 members and grew to have 535; new judicial offices are created from time to time; and new bureau chiefs are created with expansions in the bureaucracy. It would be useful to have studies into the expansion of official roles in the polity that carry with them considerable power. In Chapter III, we attempted to shed some light on the subject with respect to the state bureaucracy. Perhaps we would find from such studies that entry into the polity, for whatever reason, could not be restricted beyond a certain point, the result being a decrease in the monopolistic power of existing politicians. We may assume here, however, that entrance of additional numbers of politicians into the structure of political markets is difficult, particularly in the short run.

In this chapter we have analyzed basic political decision-making units through the use of the theory of the firm. We have attempted to show how and why these basic units behave and the societal consequences of their behavior. We argue that the polity tends to be "better off" if the markets within which the exchange behavior is conducted are decentralized, or competitive. We also suggest that it is possible to envisage the relationships of the various exchange markets that we confronted as a system of linkages between those who rank output priorities, organize input activities, and distribute the polity's output.

SIX

Exchange and Political Problems

Exchange theory has relevance for a number of issues and problems in political analysis. In the foregoing exposition, major emphasis was placed upon the theoretical and scientific value of the exchange conception as viewed from an economic perspective. We have tried to show how the concept of political exchange can be understood and how one might think about the processes and structures of political exchange. The justification for such an approach stems from the conviction that empirical political research and theory can profit, must profit, from attempts to move from a preoccupation with the sociopsychological correlates of individual and group action to a more concerted concern with interaction in the full sense of that term. An effort has been made in this book to explore insights and propositions derived from one approach to political exchange and to advance the mode of thinking and set of concepts comprising that approach. It is the task of empirical research to discover the ways in which political exchange works in the existential world, to discover more precisely what substantive political exchange markets exist, to what extent they are fundamental to the workings of a polity, who is involved in which political markets and with what consequences for the distribution of values and costs in society. Exchange theory, as we have used it, is important because it does in fact focus attention on social and political interaction and, also, because of its austerity, cohesiveness, and rigor. It is a logical structure, latent with implications (only a few of which have been touched upon in this volume) and, in the best scientific tradition, capable of generating logically related and testable propositions about human behavior. We have developed a formulation of political exchange in simple, even elementary ways, but it is a formulation easily susceptible to mathematical expression and, hence, makes possible the easy manipulation of analytical variables in the search for nonobvious but important hypotheses. These, we think, are several of the contributions that exchange theory can make to a scientific study of politics.

It is always somewhat presumptuous to prescribe a research agenda in political science. However, the present authors have reserved for another time a treatment of certain implications suggested by the theory developed in this book. One major issue concerns the need for more theoretical work on what might be described as the linkage problem in political analysis. We need to know more about "conversion" processes, or the ways in which political resources are converted into public policies, and we need such descriptions cast within the mold of the new political economy. The rich and subtle work of Parsons, Easton, Almond, and Mitchell has contributed greatly to an understanding of these processes, understood from the perspective of systems analysis.[1] The economy, lucidity, and force of economic reasoning should make possible an equally adequate and, we suspect, superior, understanding of the same issues. In the present volume, we have made some slight beginning in this direction by focusing attention on matters such as the mobilization of demands for policies, the distribution of political resources, the ranking of output priorities, the making of policy decisions, the impact of such decisions on existing structures, and the question of power. We have attempted to locate the most characteristic actors involved in these processes and have suggested the importance of decision-making rules to an understanding of political process. In fact, it is in the analysis of process, as well as exchange, that political economy may make its greatest contribution. Analysis can proceed, in the manner demonstrated in this book, both "backward" and "forward" from the polity to the broader society that exists on both the input and output boundaries of the political system. The major questions, then, that one may propose to answer with economic reasoning are ones such as: How are political resources dis-

---

[1] Talcott Parsons, "On the Concept of Political Power," *Proceedings of the American Philosophical Society,* CVII (June 1963), pp. 232–262; David Easton, *A Systems Analysis of Political Life* (New York: John Wiley & Sons, 1965); Gabriel A. Almond, "A Developmental Approach to Political Systems," *World Politics XVII* (January 1965); William C. Mitchell, *The American Polity* (New York: The Free Press of Glencoe, 1962).

tributed? How are they organized and by whom? How are demand priorities ranked in the polity? How do such rankings get translated into policy? What consequences do policy decisions and other nonpolitical events have on political resource distribution and their organization, demand priorities and, therefore, on subsequent policy decisions? And, prior to all of this, what is the distribution of tastes and preferences in the polity? Finally, what are the decision-making rules of the polity, and what is the structure of its political exchange markets?

To answer such theoretical issues will mean, necessarily, a reorganization of much empirical research. There is a requirement for more research into the actual operations of important micropolitical structures. Such structures need to be identified, classified, and their processes studied in exchange terms; that is, political conduct and performance must be analyzed from a genuinely interactional perspective, and the findings of research must be reflected in the theoretical statements of exchange theory. We have no doubt that such research would produce new behavioral propositions that would, to some extent, modify the behavioral postulates suggested in our present formulation. But that the theory has such a capability is itself evidence of its usefulness. And, finally, there is a need for more work on the further adaptability of the economists' models to both theoretical and empirical political science.

Several problems that necessarily confront any theory of political exchange have been deliberately avoided in this essay, not because they are unimportant, but because it seems preferable at this stage in the development of exchange theory to focus on the potentialities of the idea rather than upon its deficiencies. This approach—the method of the strong case, if not the alternative error—is a reasonable one in the early stages of theory-building. It is necessary, however, to give the alternative position its due. Exchange theory clearly departs from that part of contemporary social theory in which social systems are viewed as the result of shared beliefs, aspirations, and values. (On the other hand, exchange theory is quite compatible with, for example, those Marxists social scientists who have tended to view society as a bundle of antagonistic groups or classes that maintain interrelationships, however temporary, either for reasons of self-interest or, what amounts to the same thing, lack of alternatives.)

"Consensus" theory and exchange theory explain, from different perspectives, the same phenomena, or at least much of the same phenomena. Group action may emerge from the "irrational" processes of cultural events that produce people who respond similarly, or differently, to particular symbols and social circumstances in ways not necessarily, presumably, consistent with the self-interest of individual people. Blau, for example, would exclude these sorts of behaviors from the exchange conception, a conception which, of course, focuses upon rational individual action. Homans, on the other hand, would include ostensibly "irrational" social interaction in a theory of social exchange, arguing that such behavior is always an index of some chosen and preferred state.[2] For our part, we side with Homans on this issue. It is impressive to witness, for example, how frequently "irrational" political ideas (say bourgeois explanations of politics, which can be demonstrated to be objectively and "rationally" false) coincide with the self-interest of the individual, group, or class which holds them. Of course, to use the term *rational* is not to ascribe to human beings capacities that they do not possess. There are "cognitive limits on rationality" and, as Lindblom and Braybrook suggest, decision-making is often both disjointed and incremental rather than integrated and comprehensive.[3] But, within these limits, political exchanges do occur; people do make choices, and, we suggest, their decisions are frequently self-interested as we defined that term.[4] All of this must be apprehended theoretically; exchange theory of the economic variety constitutes one such method of apprehension.

Perhaps the second most frequently made criticism of economic exchange theories as applied to politics is that such theories deny, or at least overlook, the role of power in politics. Power presumably refers to some undimensional or asymmetrical action involving at least two parties. Thus, power, it is said, cannot be conceived of in exchange terms by definition since no exchange occurs in a power relationship—there are only "winners" (the powerful) and "losers" (the powerless) and no two-way distribution of rewards and costs. Without taking up the question of the "power of power" as an analytical concept,[5] it seems clear that such a view is derived, at least in part, from an inadequate appreciation of economic theory and its expression of exchange relationships. Power as usefully defined is observable in many, indeed in most, political exchange relationships. This is a fact we emphasized strongly in Chapters IV and V. The whole conception of market structure is designed to determine precisely the degrees of power that

[2] For a discussion of these two views, see Walter Buckley, *Sociology and Modern Systems Theory*, (Englewood Cliffs, N.J.: Prentice-Hall, 1967), pp. 105–113. For the original treatments, see Peter Blau, *Exchange and Power in Social Life* (New York: John Wiley & Sons, 1964), and George C. Homans, *Social Behavior: Its Elementary Forms* (New York: Harcourt, Brace & World, 1961).

[3] Charles E. Lindblom and David Braybrooke, *A Strategy of Decision* (New York: The Free Press of Glencoe, 1963). Also see Charles E. Lindblom, *The Intelligence of Democracy: Decision-Making Through Mutual Adjustment* (New York: The Free Press of Glencoe, 1965).

[4] It is a mistake to regard this notion as merely tautological; it is extremely useful in predicting behavior given other knowledge about an actor's state. See Anthony Downs, *Inside Bureaucracy* (Washington, D.C.: Public Affairs Press, 1965), pp. 81–82.

[5] James March, "The Power of Power," in David Easton (ed.), *Varieties of Political Theory* (Englewood Cliffs, N.J.: Prentice-Hall, 1963), pp. 39–70.

exist among members to any exchange. We have pointed out earlier the nature of this relationship; its importance deserves reiteration here. Indeed, the degree of "freedom" in any political exchange is a point that introduces a major issue in normative as well as scientific political theory. To raise the question of power and freedom in exchange processes is really to raise the question of democracy and competitiveness.

It was of course no accident that competitive economic systems emerged in the West together with competitive political systems. While often romanticized by both apologists and the naïve, the nineteenth and early twentieth centuries were characterized, in Anglo-American and some other societies, by reasonably high levels of competition in both economy and polity. The marketplace and the political arena, at least ideologically and rhetorically, were open to entry by all. Access to economics and politics was ostensibly, and to some extent actually, guaranteed, and, in some sectors, both political and economic power were diffused among large numbers of people. In economics, of course, the free enterprise ideology as developed by liberal economists such as Smith, Ricardo, and Malthus explained, or perhaps rationalized, the processes of economic events. In politics, the philosophies of Locke, Jefferson, and Mill undertook to explain or rationalize the diffusion of political power. Power in both spheres was viewed as having shifted from the sovereignty of the monarch or a class to the sovereignty of the individual. In the political system, equality was established by the universal franchise (to be meaningfully exercised in a framework of competitive politics); in economics, competitive markets were to allocate to all participants precisely what they deserved based upon widely available economic resources.

The theorists of these positions were not, of course, unanimous in their views (e.g., Ricardo's enmity toward the landowners' unearned income) nor particularly naïve concerning the extent to which real events corresponded to hopes expressed in their writings. But power was diffused, and competition did occur in a number of relevant ways. Competitive politics and economics produced, or, it was thought, would produce, democracy in both the countinghouse and the courthouse. Social policy would reflect not the interests of an elite, but the aggregate intentions of consumers and citizens. Consumers would vote rationally in the free marketplace for goods and services, and citizens would vote rationally in the voting booth for public policies. None of this was, or is, a very apt description of economic and political society, but the description did provide one of the most consistent and appealing normative theories of democracy ever developed. It is certainly superior, given most reasonable criteria, to the popular theories of pluralism or polyarchy that lead logically to either stalemate or minority rule.

The theory of political exchange posited in this volume does not assume the existence of viable competition in the traditional sense of that term. One may, however, prefer a polity in which political resources are as widely and equitably distributed as possible and in which political markets are open, competitive, and responsive to the needs, demands, and interests of individual citizens. Just as in the economy, there are still remnants and enclaves of competitive political markets, but it may well be that the crucial centers of political decision-making are becoming relatively concentrated and more or less closed to all but a few people. One would want to know precisely how responsive to demands autonomously generated by individual citizens the political system is. Just as bourgeois democracy and *laissez-faire* capitalism developed together historically, so, conceivably, have monopoly capitalism and monopolistic political elites developed in our own time.

Although it is not our purpose here to discuss the normative implications of exchange theory or the new political economy, it is well to point out, then, that in addition to assisting in the scientific task of identification, classification, and examination of political structures and processes, political exchange theory has important normative implications. Exchange theory will undoubtedly contribute to an empirical theory of democracy.

An economic theory of political exchange makes it possible to stipulate empirically and rigorously the requirements of open, democratic, and competitive politics, and provides criteria against which one may measure the extent to which a society conforms to, or deviates from, such standards.

Selected Bibliography

The following titles are intended to suggest materials which would serve as the basis for further study for those readers interested in other potential applications of economic theory to political or social analysis. The citations given in Section I below explain more fully the microeconomic concepts which we have used in this book. The list, of course, by no means exhausts the sources available, but should serve to introduce political and other social theorists who are not familiar with economic theory to economic thinking at three levels—introductory, intermediate, and advanced. Interested students may begin their reading at whatever level is most appropriate. In addition, we urge the reader to examine the materials cited in Section II below, which bear more directly on, and should serve as an introduction to, the issues of the "new political economy." Some of this literature requires a grounding in economics; in those cases, we suggest that the literature of political economy will be most easily accessible after perusing some of the titles in Section I.

Finally, we caution the reader that there are a great many issues in the new political economy which we have not touched upon in this book nor cited very extensively in this bibliography. Voting paradoxes, public finance, budgeting processes, public attitudes toward monetary and fiscal policy, game theory, and related issues are all logically part of this revived academic topic. The new political economy is as large a subject as political sociology. Our conceptions form only a small part of a much larger whole now being explored.

I. ECONOMIC THEORY

Introductory Books

Bernhard, Richard C., *Economics,* Chapter 12–14. Boston: D. C. Heath, 1954.

Henderson, Hubert, *Supply and Demand,* Chapter 2. Chicago: The University of Chicago Press, 1958.

McConnell, Campbell R., *Economics.* 3rd ed. New York: McGraw-Hill, 1966.

Ranlett, John G. and William I. Davisson, *An Introduction to Microeconomic Theory.* New York: Harcourt, Brace & World, 1965.

Reynolds, Lloyd G., *Economics,* Chapters 1–9. Homewood: Richard D. Irwin, 1966.

Samuelson, Paul A., *Economics,* Chapter 4 and Parts 3–4. 7th ed. New York: McGraw-Hill, 1967.

Warner, Aaron W. and Victor R. Fuchs, *Concepts and Cases in Economic Analysis,* pp. 41–62, 79–82, 94–115. New York: Harcourt, Brace & World, 1958.

Intermediate Books

Bain, Joe S., *Pricing, Distribution, and Employment.* New York: Henry Holt, 1953.

Boulding, Kenneth E., *Economic Analysis.* 3rd ed. New York: Harper & Row, 1955.

Chamberlin, Edward H., *The Theory of Monopolistic Competition.* 7th ed. Cambridge: Harvard University Press, 1956.

Ferguson, Charles, *Microeconomic Theory.* Homewood: Richard D. Irwin, 1966.

Hicks, John R., *Value and Capital,* Chapters 1–2. 7th ed. Oxford, England: The Clarendon Press, 1946.

Leftwich, Richard H., *The Price System and Resource Allocation.* New York: Holt, Rinehart & Winston, 1965.

Machlup, Fritz, *The Economics of Sellers' Competition,* Chapters 4, 5, 7, 10, 11, 16. Baltimore: The Johns Hopkins Press, 1952.

Robinson, Joan, *The Economics of Imperfect Competition.* London: Macmillan, 1933.

Ryan, W. J. L., *Price Theory.* London: Macmillan, 1958.

Stigler, George J., *The Theory of Price.* New York: Macmillan, 1966.

Advanced Books

Baumol, William J., *Economic Theory and Operations Analysis,* Chapters 9–16. Englewood Cliffs, N.J.: Prentice-Hall, 1965.

Cohen, Kalman J. and Richard M. Cyert, *The Theory of the Firm.* Englewood Cliffs, N.J.: Prentice-Hall, 1965.

Little, I. M. D., *A Critique of Welfare Economics,* Chapters 1–9. London: Oxford University Press, 1958.

Reder, Melvin, *Studies in the Theory of Welfare Economics.* New York: Columbia University Press, 1947.

Rothenberg, Jerome, *The Measurement of Social Welfare.* Englewood Cliffs, N.J.: Prentice-Hall, 1961.

II. POLITICAL ECONOMY

The best summary statement on the prospects for, and the requirements of, the new political economy is to be found in William C. Mitchell's "The Shape of Political Theory to Come: From Political Sociology to Political Economy," *American Behavioral Scientist,* XI (Nov.–Dec., 1967), pp. 8–37.

Arrow, Kenneth, *Social Choice and Individual Values.* New York: John Wiley & Sons, 1951.

Barry, Brian, *Political Argument.* New York: The Humanities Press, 1965.

Baumol, William J., *Welfare Economics and the Theory of the State.* Cambridge: Harvard University Press, 1952.

Black, Duncan, *The Theory of Committees and Elections.* Cambridge: Cambridge University Press, 1958.

———— and R. A. Newing, *Committee Decisions with Complementary Valuation.* London: William Hodge, 1951.

Blau, Peter, *Exchange and Power in Social Life.* New York: John Wiley & Sons, 1964.

Bowen, Howard, *Toward Social Economy.* New York: Rinehart, 1948.

Breton, Albert, "A Theory of the Demand for Public Goods," *Canadian Journal of Economics and Political Science,* XXXII (Nov., 1966), pp. 455–467.

Buchanan, James, *Fiscal Theory and Political Economy.* Chapel Hill: The University of North Carolina Press, 1960.

————, "Individual Choice in Voting and the Market," *Journal of Political Economy,* LVII (1954), pp. 334–343.

————, "An Individualistic Theory of Political Process," *Varieties of Political Theory,* ed. David Easton, pp. 25–37. Englewood Cliffs, N.J.: Prentice-Hall, Inc., 1966.

————, "Positive Economics, Welfare Economics, and Political Economy," *Journal of Law and Economics,* II (1959), pp. 124–138.

————, *Public Finance in Democratic Process.* Chapel Hill: The University of North Carolina Press, 1967.

————, "The Relevance of Pareto Optimality," *Journal of Conflict Resolution,* VI (Dec., 1962), pp. 341–354.

———, "Social Choice, Democracy, and Free Markets," *Journal of Political Economy*, LXII (April, 1954), pp. 114–123.

——— and Gordon Tullock, *The Calculus of Consent: Logical Foundations of Constitutional Democracy*. Ann Arbor: University of Michigan Press, 1962.

——— and M. Z. Kafoglis, "A Note on Public Goods Supply," *The American Economic Review*, LIII (June, 1963), pp. 403–414.

Casstevens, Thomas W., "A Theorem about Voting," *American Political Science Review*, LXII (March, 1968), pp. 205–207.

Catlin, George E. G. *The Science and Method of Politics*. London: George Allen and Unwin, 1927.

———, *A Study of the Principles of Politics*. London: George Allen and Unwin, 1930.

———, *Systematic Politics*. Toronto: University of Toronto Press, 1962.

Coleman, James S., "Foundations of a Theory of Collective Decisions," *The American Journal of Sociology*, LXXI (May, 1966), pp. 615–627.

Colm, Gerhard, "Theory of Public Expenditure," *Annals*, CLXXXIII (Jan., 1936), pp. 1–11.

Dahl, Robert A. and Charles E. Lindblom, *Politics, Economics, and Welfare*. New York: Harper & Bros., 1953.

Downs, Anthony, "In Defense of Majority Voting," *Journal of Political Economy*, LXIX (April, 1961), pp. 192–199.

———, *An Economic Theory of Democracy*. New York: Harper & Bros., 1957.

———, *Inside Bureaucracy*. Boston: Little, Brown, 1967.

———, "Why the Government Budget is Too Small in a Democracy," *World Politics*, XII (July, 1960), pp. 541–563.

Garvey, Gerald, "The Theory of Party Equilibrium," *The American Political Science Review*, LX (March, 1966), pp. 29–38.

Head, John G., "Public Goods and Public Policy," *Public Finance*, XVII (1962), pp. 197–219.

Hines, Lawrence G., "The Hazards of Benefit-Cost Analysis as a Guide to Public Investment Policy," *Public Finance*, XVII (1962), pp. 101–117.

Hirschman, Albert O., *Journeys Toward Progress*. New York: Twentieth Century Fund, 1963.

Homans, George C., "Social Behavior as Exchange," *The Journal of Sociology*, LXIII (May, 1958), pp. 597–606.

———, *Social Behavior: Its Elementary Forms*. New York: Harcourt, Brace & World, 1961.

Hotelling, Harold, "Stability in Competition," *The Economic Journal*, XXXIX (1929), pp. 41–57.

Lindblom, Charles E., *The Intelligence of Democracy: Decision-Making Through Mutual Adjustment*. New York: The Free Press of Glencoe, 1965.

——— and David Braybrooke, *A Strategy of Decision*. New York: The Free Press of Glencoe, 1963.

March, James G., "The Business Firm as a Political Coalition," *Journal of Politics,* XXIV (Nov., 1962), pp. 662–678.

Margolis, Julius, "A Comment on the Pure Theory of Public Expenditure," *Review of Economics and Statistics,* XXXVII (Nov., 1955), pp. 347–349.

May, K. O., "A Set of Independent Necessary and Sufficient Conditions for Simple Majority Decisions," *Econometrica,* XX (Oct., 1952), pp. 680–684.

Mitchell, William C., *Sociological Analysis and Politics.* Englewood Cliffs, N.J.: Prentice-Hall, 1967, Chapter 4.

Musgrave, Richard, *The Theory of Public Finance.* New York: McGraw-Hill, 1959.

Oliver, Henry, "Attitudes Toward Market and Political Self-Interest," *Ethics,* LXV (1955), pp. 171–180.

Olson, Mancur, *The Logic of Collective Action.* Cambridge: Harvard University Press, 1965.

Parsons, Talcott, *Sociological Theory and Modern Society.* New York: The Free Press, 1967.

Pennock, Roland, "Federal and Unitary Government—Disharmony and Frustration," *Behavioral Science,* IV (April, 1959), pp. 147–157.

Polanyi, Michael, *The Logic of Liberty.* Chicago: University of Chicago Press, 1951.

Riker, William, *The Theory of Political Coalitions.* New Haven: Yale University Press, 1962.

————, "Voting and the Summation of Preferences: An Interpretative Bibliographical Review of Selected Developments During the Last Decade," *American Political Science Review,* LV (Dec., 1961), pp. 900–911.

———— and Peter C. Ordeshook, "A Theory of the Calculus of Voting," *American Political Science Review,* LXII (March, 1968), pp. 25–42.

———— and Ronald Schaps, "Disharmony in Federal Government," *Behavioral Science,* II (1957), pp. 276–290.

Samuelson, Paul A., "Diagrammatic Exposition of a Theory of Public Expenditure," *Review of Economics and Statistics,* XXXVII (Nov., 1955), pp. 350–356.

————, "The Pure Theory of Public Expenditure," *Review of Economics and Statistics,* XXXVI (1954), pp. 387–389.

Schneider, Eugene V. and Sherman Krupp, "An Illustration of Analytical Theory in Sociology: The Application of the Economic Theory of Choice to Non-economic Variables," *The American Journal of Sociology,* LXX (May, 1965), pp. 695–703.

Shubik, Martin, "Approaches to the Study of Decision-Making Relevant to the Firm," *Journal of Business,* XXXIV (April, 1961), pp. 101–118.

Stigler, George J., "The Tenable Range of Functions of Local Government," *Federal Expenditure Policy for Economic Growth and Stability* (Washington, D.C.: Joint Economic Committee, 1957), pp. 213–216.

Tullock, Gordon, "Entry Barriers in Politics," *American Economic Review: Papers and Proceedings,* LV (May, 1965), pp. 458–466.

Tullock, Gordon, ed., *Papers on Non-Market Decision Making*. Charlottesville, Va.: Thomas Jefferson Center for Political Economy, University of Virginia, 1966.

————, *The Politics of Bureaucracy*. Washington, D.C.: Public Affairs Press, 1965.

————, "Reply to a Traditionalist," *Journal of Political Economy*, LXIX (April, 1961), pp. 200–203.

————, *Toward a Mathematics of Politics*. Ann Arbor: University of Michigan Press, 1967.

Thibaut, John W. and Harold H. Kelley, *The Social Psychology of Groups*. New York: John Wiley & Sons, 1959.

Tiebout, Charles M., "A Pure Theory of Local Expenditure," *Journal of Political Economy*, LXIV (Oct., 1956), pp. 416–424.

Williams, Allen, "The Optimal Provision of Public Goods in a System of Local Government," *Journal of Political Economy*, LXXIV (Feb., 1966), pp. 18–33.

Wilson, James Q. and Edward Banfield, "Voter Behavior on Municipal Public Expenditures: A Study in Rationality and Self-Interest," *The Public Economy of Urban Communities*, ed., Julian Margolis, pp. 74–91. Baltimore: Johns Hopkins University Press, 1965.

Zetterberg, Hans L., *On Theory and Verification in Sociology*. Totowa, N.J.: The Bedminster Press, 1963.

Index

127